PEG E. GORSON
10155 Collins Avenue
Bal Harbour, FL 33154

BILLY BALDWIN

decorates

BILLY BALDWIN decorates

by

Billy Baldwin

A House & Garden Book
HOLT, RINEHART AND WINSTON
New York Chicago San Francisco

While sincere thanks are due to a great number of people who have contributed their knowledge and skills to what you see in this book, a few special debts are owed to *House & Garden* editors for the existence of the book itself: to Mary Jane Pool, Editor-in-Chief, for planning and editing; to Miki Denhof, Associate Editor, for design and typography; to Coralee Leon, Contributing Editor, for editing the text and captions; and to Horst for the photographs (with the exceptions noted below).

B. B.

Photographs other than those by Horst: page 42 Tom Leonard; 46-47, 150-151, 154-155, 158-159-160-161-162-163-164-165 Howard Graff; 48-49, 195-196-197-198-199-200-201 William Grigsby; 133, 182-183-184-185-187-189 Andre Kertesz; 166-167 Norman Parkinson. Drawings 102-103 Henry Koehler; 186-188 Mary Faulconer. Floor Plans 110-111-112-113 Brotman. The endpapers are reproductions of "Foliage," a Woodson Wallpaper.

The author and the editors want to express their particular thanks to Vogue and to House Beautiful for permission to reprint illustrations that originally appeared on their pages.

Published, December, 1972
Second Printing, February, 1973

For
Ruby Ross Wood

CONTENTS

BILLY BALDWIN

by CLEVELAND AMORY

Every woman in America thinks she is a born interior decorator. They all say, 'I want to give you complete freedom but . . . .' My whole life has been one long battle against those 'buts,'" said William Baldwin of the decorating firm of Baldwin, Martin & Smith, in New York.

"Billy is small," his first boss, the late Ruby Ross Wood, once said, "but his sting is deep"–and to prove it she sent him a chest-of-drawers with bees all over it. Mrs. Wood was also exasperated with Billy's continual running. "Learn to walk," she said. But Billy hasn't. The day I interviewed him, he had just been arrested–for jay-running.

When In interior people get together, Billy's the Kid. The range of his work is wide–from Cole Porter's apartment high in New York's Waldorf Towers to Whitney Warren's house on Telegraph Hill in San Francisco, from his own studio apartment in New York's East Sixties to a villa in Mallorca for the Gilbert Millers, from the archconservative Round Hill

Club in Greenwich, Connecticut, to the archrevolutionary hairdressing salon of Manhattan's Mr. Kenneth. He has done a house for a woman who wanted "everything to show" and "nothing in it that had ever been done before," and he has also done a hideaway apartment for the mistress of a murderer. For some of his more run-of-the-millionaire clients, he has done as many as four houses.

"But," he said, using a "but" of the "buts" he battles, "if you can tell I did a house, I didn't. The essence of the relationship between client and decorator must be *we*." The bugaboo here is that it's often a very difficult *we*. And Baldwin, who is normally a happy person, is not made more so on the one-to-a-hundred chance that a client does say, "I know nothing," at the beginning. "I don't like that," Baldwin said, "because it's carte blanche and I hate carte blanche. It makes it almost impossible to reproduce the personal, and if there's one thing decorating is, it's personal. The worst thing any decorator can do is to give you the feeling that you're walking around in someone else's house." Warming to his task, Billy added, "The whole business has gone berserk. There's an absurd overemphasis on decoration. Decorating is not an end in itself–in fact if it turns out to be that, it is the end. Take as simple a thing as a chair. A chair, for God's sake, is to sit in. If your hostess gives you the look that makes you feel you shouldn't sit in it, it should go. The only place I'll permit a chair like that is in a bedroom and rarely there. If it's worth anything it should go to a museum. If it's not, it should go in the ash can. And speaking of ash cans, take ashtrays. An ashtray is for ashes. People who have ashtrays they are afraid are going to be harmed by using should put them somewhere else and go to the corner drugstore and get some others."

On the one hand a stern believer that uniformity is the death of individuality, Baldwin is equally stern on the subject of the novelty of today being the bad taste of tomorrow. "Décor must be, as the French say, *séant*, or suitable," he said.

"Another enemy," Baldwin said, "is the plain and simple matter of too much money. I can't tell you how many people I know who won't buy something unless it's expensive. I know it isn't good business, but I tell them what I think anyway. I think an unpleasant atmosphere results from the entry into the obviously 'rich' room–the kind that makes you feel you're caught right in the middle between the devil of a museum and the deep sea of the *embarras de richesse*. And one thing you can say for Southern women–they're far less guilty on this score than Northerners."

Baldwin then brought up art. "I have far too much respect for art to reduce it to decoration. A picture should never be bought to be a part of decoration. In fact, if a picture isn't loved for itself and by the person who buys it, it shouldn't be bought at all. I don't think anyone has a right to possess anything he doesn't love–art or anything else."

At the same time, Baldwin sees the decorator as a kind of artist–only a special kind of artist, a portrait painter. "I know portrait painters who won't paint people they don't like," he said, "and I at least try not to decorate for people I don't like. After all, we're back to that *we* again. I help. I assist. I do not do. I've never solicited a job in my life. People come to me the way they do to a doctor or a lawyer–there must be trust. The quickest way not to get their money's worth is for them not to trust their decorator."

Although Baldwin treasures his few men clients–"if for no other reason," he said, "because they don't change their minds so often" –they are worse than women when it comes to trust. Most men distrust decorators on sight. As for giving credit after the job is done, however, men are better. "Many women would like to credit their decorator, but they feel they can't. And now we're back to that original born-decorator thing."

Actually, Baldwin believes there are only two or three women in each city who are really born decorators–who are born, as he puts it, "with that extra thing of flair and personal flavor. They are the independents. They feel no pressure of the dictates of a decorator."

Baldwin came under the influence of four such women, and he is only too happy to credit them. The first was Dr. Claribel Cone, one of the famous Cone sisters of Baltimore. He was taken to her apartment when he was ten years old. "I can remember it just as if it were yesterday," he said. "It was there I first saw a Matisse. It opened the door of freedom for me." From that day on whenever his mother went shopping to choose materials or anything like that, she always took Billy along–to ask him about color. "I can't remember a single occasion," he said, "when she didn't."

Baldwin's father was an insurance man who sent Billy to Gilman and Princeton. At Princeton he became so interested in architecture and decoration–"and spent so much time in New York at museums and galleries and things"–that he never bothered to graduate. After Princeton, he returned to Baltimore, where he came under the great influence of Mrs. John W. Garrett. At her famous "Evergreen House," Billy remembers seeing twenty-four Raoul Dufy watercolors as well as the first Picasso he actually saw on someone's wall. The Garrett house had not only a private theater done by Bakst, the great colorist for the Russian ballet, but also a wing of the house all of red lacquer and Chinese furniture. "Alice Garrett," he said, "was the second stop of my emancipation. She took my mind right out of Maryland and jumped me from eighteenth-century England into the modern Continental world."

His third great influence, and the third step of his emancipation, was the beginning of his long friendship with Pauline Fairfax Potter, now the Baroness Philippe de Rothschild. "When I first knew Pauline," he said, "she had a small house in an unfashionable section of Richmond Street with no money. At seventeen her flower arrangements were fantastic– and her table decorations, too. She could take a few family possessions, a few bits of Chippendale, and somehow take them right out of the stereotype. Her great gift was the unconventional use of conventional things."

In those days, decorators always felt the necessity of pairs–a pair of chairs, a pair of lamps, a pair of practically everything but the decorators themselves. Pairs were, in fact, decorators' signatures. "Pauline," Baldwin said, "even in that little house, made me aware of the importance of space, of the beauty of asymmetry, of the wisdom of waiting."

His first major job–one that attracted the attention of Ruby Ross Wood and eventually brought him to New York–was the house he decorated for Baltimore's Mrs. Thomas Symington. "I'd really done nothing up to then," he said, "but Edith gave me everything to play with–Italian beds, Spanish chairs, Portuguese tables."

The late Mrs. Wood, born in Georgia, was, of course, the woman who headed the first department of decoration in any department store–the famous "Au Quatrième" on the New York Wanamaker's fourth floor. In addition, Mrs. Wood was the ghostwriter of the Elsie de Wolfe Mendl book, *The House in Good Taste.* For Baldwin–in an era when everybody was afraid of de Wolfe, in this case de Wolfe being de Elsie–Mrs. Wood marked the fourth and final step in his emancipation. "Ruby had three credos," he said, "and all three of them were unbelievably simple. First, the personal–she never let you lose sight of the personal in decorating. Second, comfort. Her great and guiding rule was to arrange beautiful things comfortably. Third and last, the new. She made you aware of the importance of the new design or the new color or the new whatever–this, she used to say, 'keeps your mind young'–but she also made you select only what you considered best and always cast aside the novelty."

At the beginning, Baldwin remembers he had several failures–one stands out in his mind as especially awful: "I was color mad. I did one four-room apartment that was the all-time horror–one room blue, one green, one red, and one yellow. There was no restraint, no discipline, and no continuity. The whole place looked like an Easter egg hunt."

Now, pressed to name what he considers the most outstanding of his accomplishments, he chooses Cole Porter's apartment in the Waldorf Towers. From the beginning this presented seemingly insuperable problems: to install in a New York apartment, and in a hotel apartment at that, Linda Porter's great collection of French furniture, which she had first in the Rue Monsieur in Paris and then at her house in Williamstown. "At Williamstown," Baldwin said, "Cole even had a separate house. He had about as much personal connection with Linda's furniture as I did. My job was to reassemble this personal collection after Linda died and somehow reidentify it with a change of color from the ultrafeminine taste of Linda to the bachelor taste of Cole. What I had to do, for example, was to take that fabulous Chinese wallpaper from Linda's drawing room [Billy emphasizes the words] to Cole's living room."

Porter gave him carte blanche–but with one exception. "Don't forget," he said, "I'm Broadway." Baldwin did not forget. And if he tried to restore the atmosphere of Paris in the twenties (there was even a dark green Elsie de Wolfe Mendl memorial guest room), there was also a brass library. But Porter asked for something else, too–a red bed. ("And," added Baldwin, "it was a riot of red.") There were, however, other injunctions, too. "I do not want," Porter told him, "an elaborate installation to hide my television any more than I want slipcovers for my pianos." Since Porter entertained primarily at lunch, the living room had to be at its best at the lunch hour, and since Porter was left-handed, all the vast engineering network of the apartment–the air conditioners, hi-fi, tape recorder, et cetera– had to be operated from switches placed to the left of Porter's favorite chairs. Finally, since Porter hated bells, everywhere in the apartment there were bulbs only–red for the front door, white for the back door, and blue for the telephone.

The apartment, in fact, was so close to perfection that more than one visitor wanted one just like it. Once, in fact, not one but two Broadway producers commissioned Baldwin to do one like it for each of them. "The very fact they wanted something just like anyone else's ought to have been enough of a warning for me," Baldwin said. "But really, just like Cole's–I 14 don't know how I could have been that stupid. And, of course, halfway along they wanted something else–it was much too subtle for them." This kind of story, however, is rare for Baldwin–as is his story of finishing in record time an apartment for the mistress of a convicted murderer–a man who was to get two days off. Only once after he finished the job did Baldwin ever see or hear from the woman again. One day, as he was shopping in Park & Tilford, someone came up behind to press something into his back. Turning around and seeing the woman, Baldwin was extremely agitated, but in a moment she was gone. Not, however, before pressing into his hand something he has always treasured–a candy heart.

"I have to live in a tomb of silence," he added. "I could list a hundred names of people everybody thinks are wonderful who, when you work for them, are really . . . well, I won't use the word. I've had some of the most famous names in this country say the most incredible things to me. I had one woman say she wanted a bed out of a material that had never been made. Another woman said she wanted her sofa to look as if old ladies had crocheted it. Another woman wanted a 'room divider' but one that had to have, she said, 'a piano, a bookcase, and a bar with hot and cold running water.'" Once, after perhaps Baldwin's most difficult failure (the woman had called one of his most remarkable rooms a "Call Me Madam room"), he was praised for what a friend, who knew the full story, called his "chic behavior." Baldwin replied, "It's not chic behavior. It's just not the American way to go around advertising your failures." Baldwin is close to being jingoistic.

"I can't tell you," he said, "how American I am. This belittling thing about America in decorating makes me so mad. I'm against the all-English house or the all-French house or the all-Spanish house–any of these must be translated into terms that suit the American Way for the America today. We can recognize and give credit where credit is due to the debt of taste we owe to Europe, but we have taste, too–in fact, we're a whole empire of taste. That is my flag, and I love to wave it."

Only your eye can tell you
what you will
be happy with.
Today, thank goodness,
we are more concerned
with the personal
than with perfection.

1
TASTE AND LOGIC IN DECORATING

TASTE AND LOGIC IN DECORATING

The logic of the eye

The final judge in decorating, as any wise decorator knows, is not the "logic of the mind, but the logic of the eye." I learned that thirty years ago—it was pointed out to me in those words by Ruby Ross Wood— and it has never failed to be true.

The logic of the eye is fascinating, and it applies in the most rudimentary stages of furnishing a room. For instance, you start out by drawing a floor plan—this is for the bone structure—to make sure the room will include everything needed and that everything will be arranged for comfort, convenience, and beauty. But even the best-laid furniture plan may not work quite so well in actuality as it does on paper. You have to be flexible so that even at this early stage, you can substitute or rearrange. Naturally I always try to see the actual room in my mind's eye, but even with the most careful planning and mental visualization, there is always the possibility of error.

Once I did a little girl's bedroom in the Placido Arango apartment in Madrid. But when I went back a year later to visit, I saw that the whole point of the room had been lost. So I had to turn it almost completely around, adding nothing, but rearranging. I have designed rooms beginning with a picture, and the picture never even got into the room. Even when floor plans have been very carefully worked out, it is always possible that when the furniture is put in place a certain chair may look better on the other side of the room. Moving it can make all the difference in the world, but you can't always see that kind of thing on paper.

When you ignore the logic of the eye, the result may be a room that is disastrously uncomfortable even though it is undeniably beautiful. I've seen too many rooms that have to be almost entirely rearranged before you can sit down. I've actually heard people ask, "May I bring up this chair?" That is absolutely awful. No room, of course, can be furnished to accommodate an indefinite number of people, but at least it can be arranged so you can inconspicuously pull up a chair without having to ask permission. Chairs should be in the right places—where they are needed. Sometimes people have a pair of perfectly beautiful antique chairs set against the wall, but if they see you going for them the look you get is lethal. Well I don't think those chairs should be there. If they are not meant to sit on, they should be in the hall.

My eye has told me, over the years, that there is even a place in decorating for nondecorating; purposely leaving out certain things when you first furnish a room so that just the right pieces can be added later. I believe, for instance, that we should always leave room for a picture or pictures. Then, when the perfect ones come along— those you simply cannot live without—the room suddenly seems to have been waiting for them, and welcomes them.

Overleaf: Down-to-earth living room in an Arizona ranch house.

furniture

The logic of the eye is often the wisest guide to choosing furniture, too. For instance, I certainly cannot conceive of a room without some well-designed, fully upholstered furniture. Apart from actual comfort, a roomful of chair and table legs looks restless. I feel, too, that a mixture of styles and periods and nationalities is what we want today: all rooms should be contemporary, a mixture of the antique and the modern. From the fantastic range of choices, your intellect and your experience can help pick out the good designs, the furniture with quality, character, and value. But only the eye can tell you which you would be happy to live with.

The eye protects us from tripping into the pitfalls to which pure intellect often leads. In scaling the furniture to fit the room, for instance, what you automatically try for is perfection—furniture that is neither too large nor too small. But I appreciate the value and vitality of overscale. (Never underscale, though. The meagerness of under-scale never seems to have any guts or style.) Even more important than knowing the rules is to know how and when to break them. I would much rather use a commode that was actually too big for the room—or a massive armoire—than something dinky looking. I would rather have a sofa that was too big if it looked terribly comfortable.

When it comes to color, the eye has to come into its own. The impressionist and postimpressionist painters liberated us from the fear of color—no longer are we limited to soft, faded tonality, and I for one am grateful. I love the strength of clear, true color with lots of white that you see in so many contemporary fabric patterns, and abstract paintings. I also love the colors of the eighteenth century—that glorious age of no compromise—brave and bold.

What I believe in and work for are rooms that express the taste of my client and fit the uses to which they will be put—rooms, in other words, that belong to him. I do not think a decorator has the right to impose a style, or to dictate the kind of atmosphere his clients should live in. The mood of a room should be personal. It might be a cluttered room full of personal memorabilia—books, photographs, needle-point-in-work—all the things that are impossible to impose, impossible to accumulate, except by the person who lives there. Or it might be a room where space abounds, surrounding every piece of furniture, every object—a room where there are only a few personal possessions, all of which count. Here the atmosphere is of cool beauty and serenity, particularly successful if some of the furnishings have eccentric personalities.

There is magic, too, in the deep-jewel-colored room, warm and mysterious, where you discover its many beauties as you sit, seduced slowly. Or in the brilliant white room, accented by clear strong color, always looking fresh and pristine. Or in the distinguished calm of the no-color room, all browns and black and white.

How can a decorator dictate that a room should be empty or cluttered or deeply colored or even filled with potpourri? He can guide, and suggest, using all his wisdom and experience. But finally the client must look to the logic of his own eye. For the ultimate result should be a room where you are surrounded by the things that really make you comfortable and happy, things that you really love—what Ruby Ross Wood called "the pleasant memorabilia of living."

21

Good taste
has no price tag

Long ago Elsie de Wolfe aptly defined good taste as "suitability! suitability! suitability!" Today the definition holds more than ever. Nothing is in good taste, regardless of its cost, unless it suits your personality and the way you live.

Still, there are always some people who are impressed by how much they pay for things, and sometimes even go as far as to tell us. For instance, those would-be sophisticates who buy Fine French Furniture not because it suits the way they live, or even because they like it, but purely out of snobbery. Price is almost totally invalid as a measure of value, especially today when everything costs so much, so often second-rate workmanship. Quite apart from that, the expensive look is just not suitable to the way most of us live, regardless of our incomes.

Quality, on the other hand, is always essential whatever the price. There is no question that a good piece of furniture is a sound investment. By good, I mean either an antique or something contemporary, beautifully designed and made. I resent spending large sums on mediocre furniture that lacks both the mellow charm of a lovely old piece and the freshness of the contemporary. I would rather use for the time being an unpainted table with a long cloth—or a table my client already owns and loves. My fellow decorators often attack me for this. "How could you possibly allow that terrible table?" they'll say to me. I tell them I couldn't possibly not allow it. I know that in a year or two, perhaps, my client may very well realize the table can be improved upon, and that is the time to change it. Meanwhile, it hasn't cost a cent to use a table she already owns, and that table has contributed far more flavor and personality to the room than some table you see everywhere. "Reproductions" are expensive, and have no value aesthetically—see how much you can get when you decide to sell—they become secondhand the moment you own them.

Another good investment is custom-made upholstered furniture. When furniture is made just for you, you can make sure the frame is of seasoned wood; you know exactly what the stuffing is made of; and you get exactly the style you want in the dimensions you need. I always recommend that upholstered furniture be covered in neutral twill—which costs about the same as muslin—then slipcovered. If a slipcover is properly made, it is indistinguishable from a permanent cover and so much easier to clean. And when the slipcovers are at the cleaners, the neutral fabric underneath looks quite presentable. Although it might seem extravagant to have one set of slipcovers for summer and another for winter, it is really economical in the long run—and so refreshing to see the room change as the seasons turn.

The old-fashioned idea that good taste calls for a consistent level of elegance has been completely exploded. If you plan the room around a few good investments, there is no reason why you can't fill in with humbler things of good design. Some people have a natural talent for mixing the very expensive with the very humble, and they do it not for lack of means, but because they do not value what they love in terms of price. Way back in the thirties, I knew a woman with marvelous taste (Pauline de Rothschild) who kept a wicker basket filled with flowers on top of a French commode fine enough to be in a museum. Now, of course, everyone does such things. But at that time, on that kind of commode, you would feel you had to have a Sèvres cachepot of enormous price. In my own apartment, I have a wicker tray sitting on top of a very good Louis XVI gilt stand, and to me the wicker seems much more charming as a top than some grand piece of marble.

Lacquer is something that always adds warmth and charm, whether it is a great Coromandel screen or the simplest contemporary Japanese lacquer box. It is at home anywhere—at ease in a palace, never too proud to be in a cottage. I know one woman who keeps a little lacquer box of absolutely no value whatsoever—a box in the prettiest shade of pale lime-green—beside a small painting of a child by Renoir. What if there is a discrepancy in their intrinsic values? If both the expensive and the inexpensive are, in their ways, first class, they can be perfectly harmonious.

Occasionally you find that something undeniably suitable happens to be out of vogue, but remember that suitability overrules fashion. I used to have wall-to-wall carpeting. When other decorators came to my apartment for the first time, they often looked aghast at it. Well why not? I admit I am not generally an advocate of wall-to-wall, but in certain cases it makes sense. My living room is small and irregular. The carpeting helped to unify the space and smooth out the angles. And it really absorbed noise, which is why I recommend it heartily for big-city bedrooms. By the same token, I think lamps should be of the simplest possible design—no overscaled lampshades, please—and not expensive. Lamps are first and last for light. This year's fashionable "art lamp" is very apt to be next year's horror.

Suitability today means things that are young, simple, easy to care for. In fabrics, I like cotton and linens. They have a certain cleanliness, a youthful freshness that's just right for today. My summer slipcovers are pale blue denim—sixty-nine cents a yard. I also have a set made of paisley cotton for winter. There is such variety in cottons—all the wonderful prints in marvelous colors—that it seems terribly old fashioned to insist on a lot of stuffy expensive materials.

Probably the main reason some people persist in confusing good taste with great expense is that they long for luxury, but they misunderstand the meaning of the word. They confuse it with grandeur. To me, luxury is something very different. Recently a woman I know bought an old farmhouse in an apple orchard near the sea. For comfort she installed a completely modern bathroom, with the tub placed by an enormous window. For luxury, she relaxes in the bath, and gazes out upon the apple orchard and the sea.

The sterility of
perfection

I know a magnificent French apartment in
New York that someone has brilliantly described as "a series of foyers leading to
nothing." How sad to see rooms so beautiful, yet so cold. You must walk through the
austere living room and out again in search of a small haven of comfort to sit in. Even
the master bedroom looks like an unwelcoming guest room.

A young client of mine expressed the same feelings another way. We were discussing his library, where he works during the evening while his wife reads or does
needlepoint. They had just returned from visiting a newly decorated house with a
library that had made them cringe with horror—shiny walnut paneling, yards and
yards of brand-new untouched books, a new desk without a trace of evidence that it
had ever been used. The young man said, "I hope you understand that we do not want
our house to be perfect." This young couple had glimpsed the awful sterility of perfection, and realized at once what I have always maintained: Nothing is interesting
unless it is personal. So their library has a superb Louis XVI desk, and sitting unashamedly beside it, an efficient filing cabinet.

Everyone has his own needs, his own preferences, his own ways of using space.
When a decorator disregards these needs, or tries to superimpose an alien personality,
he cannot bring off that wonderful warm atmosphere of a private, personal place.

I, for one, cannot imagine a fireplace without a fire burning whenever there is
the slightest excuse for it. I cannot conceive of a house in the country without dogs, or
of any house without books—the greatest decoration of all. These give a room
heart—along with lighted candles and the smell of fresh flowers, or bowls of potpourri in open windows.

There is nothing quite so boring as false refinement, or so vulgar as misplaced
elegance. I have often quoted Cole Porter, who said to me: "Please don't try to
hide my television, or make slipcovers for my piano." I had a client once who was
infuriated when I put flowers on her grand piano.

"Do you know who plays that piano?" she said. "Rubinstein! Get those
flowers off."

"Well," I replied, "does he play it every night?" It wasn't as if I had put a
Spanish shawl on it, or a crowd of photographs. How pretentious to object to
movable blossoms!

A woman whose house Elsie de Wolfe had decorated years ago always kept
twelve red roses on her hall console. Elsie had probably said, "Wouldn't it be nice to
have some red roses there," and the woman had taken it as an unalterable dictum. But

the roses never looked as if she had fallen in love with them in the florist's window. They were just furniture.

One of the greatest sterilizers of the would-be perfectionist is fashion. There's no reason for rooms and houses to change as often as hairdos and skirt lengths. All rooms should begin as outgrowths of the owner's personality, then become lovelier, more personal, and more welcoming with every year. I haven't much interest in a client who asks me what I have just done in someone else's living room, or worse yet, what the "latest trends" are. If I find that something I am doing is becoming a trend, I run from it like the plague.

A client has no one but herself to blame for a sterile, uninteresting house if she hasn't the gumption or self-assurance to assert herself. Ruby Ross Wood once took me to visit one of her clients who lived in a beautiful house with superb furniture and lots of lovely little objects and flowers around. But the woman was frantic. "I'm going out of my mind," she said. "Someone has given me this little box, and I don't know where to put it." Ruby snatched the box from her and thumped it on the first table she came to. "Put it there," she said. The woman had become so afraid of her own room, she felt everything in it had to be an arrangement.

Some people add enormously to a room in a way that no decorator ever could. They can move into a newly decorated house and make it look as if they have lived there for thirty years. And a year later, you see still more wonderful growth. I know several people with this precious knack—I work out the colors and fabric and furniture arrangement, and when everything is in place I say, "All right. Now go ahead and mess it up." Then they buy and arrange the paintings and objects, make needlepoint pillows, fix flowers, move a chair to a place where it really is more comfortable. They break up the hardness of the perfect look, and make the room their own.

The way people accumulate and display objects can add immeasurably to a room's vitality. For a decorator to go out and buy a whole collection at one fell swoop is almost an invasion of privacy. To display it formally in some ghostly lighted cabinet, as the French often do, makes me shudder. I love to see collections that have been gathered over the years kept right out in the open as the English keep them—on tables and commodes where you can see them and touch them.

A touch of wit can help a great deal to ward off the sterile look. I don't mean that a room should make you roar with laughter, but as you sit in it, you might be struck suddenly by some unexpected object, an entertaining picture, some little eccentricity of the owner. In my window there sits a foolish little wooden monkey holding a globe covered with chips of mirror that shoot sparks of sunlight all over the room. It is a very silly thing, but a good friend gave it to me and I like it. The Duke di Verdura found a little fieldstone, split it in half, and polished the insides. When you open the two halves, you discover a little green-enamel lizard that he tucked between them. It is a shock every time! Things like that are fun to collect for your own house, and delightful to come upon in someone else's. But I would never go out and buy something "funny" for a room. No object should "wink" at us.

A good friend of mine served Chinese fortune cookies at her husband's sixtieth birthday party. The wife laughed when she read her own fortune: "Your marriage will be prosperous." Next time I visited them, I happened to notice quite by accident something that struck me as the essence of making a room warm and alive. On a table sat a little glass box—a French box with gold edges, probably of great value. And there in the box, like a jewel, was that crinkled message from the fortune cookie.

The
rule breaker's
success

The first rule of decoration is that you can break almost all the other rules. A room arranged absolutely according to the book, with little *i*'s dotted and big *t*'s crossed, is all very well in its impersonal way. But the rooms that are really successful declare the owner's independence, carry the owner's signature, his very private scrawl.

It's a rule that pattern should not be played against pattern, that figured curtains need a plain wall. But nothing is more enchanting than the indoor garden that grows from flowering chintz, flowered walls, flowery needlework rugs. One of the pleasantest drawing rooms on Long Island has a flowered Bessarabian rug, all muted reds and faded greens, with furniture slipcovered in pale-green and cream flower chintz, and a flourish of books, pictures, bunches of flowers. Another handsome room, this one in town, spreads a soft ancient Oriental rug across the floor, and surprises it by overlaying another, much smaller and higher in key, in front of the little French mantel.

It's a rule that one chintz is a charmer—two's a crowd. But maybe you want to cover two chairs in chintz, and can find only enough of a fabric to cover one. Well, use it—and for the second chair use another chintz, of equal caliber but different design. No one hesitates to hang two flower paintings in the same room, so why not allow two flower chairs, like distinct and lovely bouquets?

There's a great distinction in no pattern at all. Consider a room all the dark fresh green of gardenia leaves. The walls might be highly lacquered; the curtains dull, roughly woven; the sofas and chairs covered in damask and needlework—all wearing the green, but with their own textures giving their own value to it. The variety would be subtle, but very real. And don't forget that one person puts pattern and movement into a room, and the intricacy of the design grows with the size of the party.

There's chic in repetition—a splurge of the same fabric for curtains, sofas, chairs. Don't be timid about making this an all-out effort, or your friends will suspect that you undercalculated your yardage. In Connecticut, there's a wonderful salon, its style a kind of Norwegian Louis XVI. On a polished Fontainebleau floor is ranged a levee of chairs and sofas, all painted chalk white, all covered with a pale-blue, gray, and white checked fabric. The curtains are of the same fabric, the walls are a misty gray-blue, and the effect is fabulous.

There's chic in not repeating. One very grand drawing room has walls of glowing red flock-paper, gold satin curtains, gold and white furniture—nowhere another flicker of red. And one chair in a high clear tone makes its point more conclusively if its color is not echoed. In a gray monochrome room, a chair covered in poison-green satin will lose its fine sting if the green is recalled in a pillow or two on the little gray sofa. It's superfluous to repeat the green at all, but if you must, do it in an off-shade and another medium—perhaps an emerald-green chandelier.

A few decorating principles seem safe from contradiction. When you are arranging furniture, it's always wise to put pieces of equal value together. Don't hang a contemporary painted mirror over an elegant old commode. The mirror may have its decoration virtue, but in that false position it will insult the antique, and show itself for an upstart. If you are looking for a mantel garniture, choose something that has the same quality as the mantel itself, and the picture or mirror over it. (There's a seeming exception to this rule—one lovely mantel arrangement involves a beige marble Louis XV mantel, and on it a row of purple violets in modest clay pots, reflected in a superb gilt mirror. But this makes sense, because the pots don't pretend to be more than they are; they are, in their own way, just as authentic.)

If you spend most of your decorating money on a Chippendale table or a Chinese lacquer screen, don't fill in the gaps with mediocrity. Forget the gaps for a while; just have simple slipcovers in one pretty color. Then, as you can, acquire other good pieces that are compatible with your first extravagance. Let the room grow slowly to maturity. There is "costume" decoration as well as "costume" jewelry—in itself, it may have charm, but it tends to destroy the charm of the Real Thing, if used with it.

No one object should dominate a room. A great work of art is the richest endowment a room can have, and it should be given a dominating position—but if it is really great, it will have the grace of all great things, and won't be too obtrusive. Today we don't want to be too conscious of the *mise en scène*; don't want to have curtains, chairs, paintings thrust themselves forward as topics of conversation.

It's far more important to have three rooms that are beautifully done and beautifully run than to have ten or twenty that are dreary and neglected. Some of the most distinguished buildings in the world are the little villas, pavilions, orangeries. If we live in small-scale rooms, we needn't be limited to small-style decoration. A tiny library—with boiserie and double doors—can have as much style as a ballroom, and can offer more stimulus to conversation.

Avoiding
the
unhappy medium

I remember when I was a child always hearing grown-ups singing the praises of the "happy medium." The advocates of moderation, caution, and safety-first certainly have their place in life, but in decorating they are a total bore. If you pursue the happy medium with enough determination, you will eventually compromise your room to the point where nothing is left. No life, no personality, no sparkle. The room may be perfectly arranged, with valuable furniture and a strict devotion to silk. But what you will have achieved is a banal and sterile void—a medium that is not so happy after all. Anyone can produce a perfectly tasteful, stuffed shirt of a room. All you have to do is follow the rules. Anyone can hang an impressionist and guarantee safe applause. But to get a room that sizzles with personality, you've got to take risks. A person with a real flair is a gambler at heart.

Some women actually prefer to live in a flavorless room for the sake of avoiding criticism. They are deathly afraid of making a mistake, of being ridiculed, of getting too far ahead of the Joneses. I know of one woman who threw out every idea her decorator came up with because she suspected her friends might find fault with it. She got just the room she wanted, but she didn't need a decorator. A computer could have put that room together, probably much faster and with fewer arguments and aspirins. You would find no reason to say: "How could she have allowed that monstrosity of a table?" One step out the door and you couldn't remember a thing.

Whenever I take on a job, I am confronted with a room, a budget, the tastes of the owners, and the uses to which the room will be put. So I start by presenting a furniture scheme showing scale and furniture groupings that fill the basic needs, with colors and furniture styles based on the clients' preference. But deep under the surface of the measuring tapes and swatches, something more is brewing. When I'm really enthusiastic about a job, and have a pleasant rapport with the clients, an added intangible element pervades the entire operation. I become part of my work, and sometimes the results are highly unconventional ideas that suit my clients perfectly. Some of the ideas are departures they would never think of, or if they did might be afraid to try themselves. For instance, a beautiful screen placed where one is not strictly necessary, except that it makes the room glow when the afternoon light strikes it in a certain way. Or a patterned rug on top of the plain carpet. Or a pair of extraordinary animals flanking the fireplace. Or a table designed especially for the room.

Sometimes people don't trust their own taste or mine either. One client in New York wanted her big living room to look like a room in the country: "White, white,

white." I heartily approved all she specified—modern furniture, clear colors, everything washed in light. When the room was done, it looked just the way she planned it, but to me it was rather cold looking and somehow unfinished like a low garden with nothing in the background. What the room needed, so to speak, was trees. One day I sent up a big contemporary painting and had it set on the mantel, just to get a reaction. A message was on my desk the next morning: "Will Mr. Baldwin please come and take that terrible thing away." But I could see that the painting lifted the room into a whole new dimension, so I enlisted the help of the woman's husband, who loved it, and we persuaded her to leave it for a week before making a final decision. For the first day or two she looked on the painting as some kind of gate-crasher, but by the end of the week she wouldn't part with it. In decorating as in anything else, it often takes time to make friends with something strange. Many of the woman's friends will probably react to the picture at first the way she did, for it is a painting, admittedly, with specialized appeal. But it is a wonderful one. And now she thinks it is, too.

Please don't think for a minute that I'm advocating a lot of trinkets, or novelty for its own sake. What I am advocating is the use of good sound design, but in unexpected ways. A decorator has an advantage in this respect because he has access to imports, antiques, and designer showrooms that the average person does not. If he is familiar with your tastes, he can show you a lot you might otherwise miss. But even without a decorator, you can bring some dazzle to a commonplace room. The first step is to take a deep breath. Become a bit of a daredevil. If you have some money to spend, surprise the eye with indirect lighting, an eccentric old commode, or a modern coffee table. Splurge on a painting. Or replace a period chaise longue with a voluptuously comfortable chair and ottoman in a totally unpredictable material.

If you must limit yourself to smaller changes, why not cover a big table with a scarlet felt cloth? Or a crocheted afghan? Or a bandana with a white linen square laid over it? Charm is augmented by a sense of nonpermanence. Spread a small but brilliant rug under the coffee table. Toss around some really terrific pillows, slipcovered so you can switch them on sudden whim. The trouble with many people is that they take their rooms too seriously. Play with your rooms. Mess around a little. Besides building up your talent and developing your eye, it's really great fun.

I love it when clients get daring on their own. They begin timidly: "Now I'm only thinking out loud, so don't jump on me if the idea sounds barbaric, but what if we had just one chair in black linen?" It might be realizable at once as a stroke of genius. Or perhaps it could turn out to be disastrous. If disastrous, too bad. That's part of the gamble. I've had to re-cover more than one chair at my own expense because one of my ideas turned out to be a bomb. But if the client's reaction really is right, she herself has accomplished what every decorator lives for.

With or without a decorator, it's just this kind of pizzazz that every room needs to become alive. In a house that steers clear of the happy medium, even casual visitors can sense that something good is going on. They may rave, they may applaud, they may laugh, they may be shocked. But they'll never, ever yawn.

IN ARIZONA,
A HOUSE WITH THE ROMANCE
OF A SPANISH HILL TOWN

"The concept of the architecture," wrote a client of mine about a new house she and her husband were building in the mountains of southern Arizona, "was to create the illusion that we had found a tiny old Spanish hill town and, by connecting all the parts, created a house. We asked that the interior have a slightly traditional atmosphere, and that it be turned inward from the surrounding vastness that is all too apparent outside. This house must lure me to Arizona. Just the horses will lure my husband." Letters like this were my real guides in decorating. My clients, after one session with their architects, the brilliant firm of Ford, Powell, and Carson of San Antonio, left me quietly, beautifully alone.

*W*hen I saw the completed structure, above, my impression was exactly that of coming upon a sleepy little town in the hills of Spain. From the entrance court, the house seems low and nestled in the folds of the hill. To quote my clients: "The different levels of the house and terraces give it a medieval feeling. Rather than shooting away from the hill, the house hugs it. The terrace pergolas soften the view, and small traditional windows create a cloistered quality that is terribly attractive in these God-like regions. And they are God-like!"

*T*he ceilings of the house are its
triumph—beamed and cross-
beamed like a handsome fortress.
All the floors are paved with pinky-
beige Mexican tiles. ("The architect is very good at pulling up old
tile roads in Mexico and carrying
them across the border.") In the
living room, there is as much sensual texture and visual calm as
possible. Colors are tawny, quiet,
and warm—the most cheerful
colors of the landscape rather than
some high-toned intrusion. Two
sofas are covered in earth-colored
suede, four chairs in fat-weave
white linen, and the walls are the
only color they ever could be.
White. The swimming pool, right,
we painted the color of lapis lazuli.

In the dining room, right, the colors are soft and relaxing, with the only real smash a terrific red painting by Stamos. Because of the upward slope of the ceiling, I felt that the table should edge toward the lower, more intimate side of the room. There is no chandelier, just three very, very soft ceiling spots, and at night, of course, candlelight. For warmth and sound control, the floor is brick-patterned wood, the one exception to tile in the house. The rug is an ancient Kara-bagh, and a marvel. Outdoor lunching and dining are done on a terrace, above, with a trestle table and cushionless benches. You can swim up to the last second and come dripping to the table. In the entrance hall, left, four chairs are covered in the very velvet used in Siena for costumes for the famous Palio, and the ceiling soars to the highest point of the house and a little square window like the eye of Heaven.

On the pool terrace, below, *the decorating is mostly taken care of by the view, but for the* master bedroom and bath, left and above, *both within the same four walls, I tried to create something of a sheik's tent in the Sahara: enveloping, sensuous, removed from the slightly austere surroundings. The single strong art-nouveauish pattern of the wallpaper and fabric was taken from a Klimt painting. Still in natural earth colors with the addition of some sky, it has all the* warmth and radiance of a paisley without its obviousness. The windows don't have curtains, but the bed does, and they all draw to keep out the violent Arizona dawn. For more tactile pleasures, there are a linen-velvet sofa and slipper chairs in the color of rich clay. And everything that isn't covered with wallpaper is made of marble—tub platform, stall shower, toilet and bidet enclosure, the countertops on cabinets flanking an Italian chest. The pale tile floors are smooth and cool.*

All rooms should begin
as an outgrowth
of your own personality,
then become more personal,
and more welcoming
with every year.
You should never
be so aware of a room
that it comes between you and
the person you are with.
That's not decoration,
it's interference.

2
ROOMS
TO
LIVE IN

ROOMS TO LIVE IN

Highways of the house— halls and hallways

In Mrs. Wolcott Blair's Georgian house on Long Island, the first room you enter, as in numerous other houses, is a big square space called the hall. But in place of the usual impersonal, sparsely furnished chilliness that's enough to make you shiver as you take off your coat, there are rugs, wonderful chintz-covered furniture, and a blazing fire in the fireplace. It's a pleasure not only to linger as you greet your hostess, but also, in certain seasons and at certain times of day, to be served tea or cocktails there. The English would call such a room the living hall—a place where the mail is brought to the central table and perhaps read by the fire, where the piano is played and the tennis rackets or golf clubs get left on a bench or hatrack near the entrance. No matter how you use it, when a hall is lived in, a magic thing happens—the heartbeat of the house begins at the front door.

When you decorate such a hall, you can be a lot more adventurous with color and pattern than in other rooms. After all, no matter how comfortable you make it, you won't be sitting there all day. In an old clapboard farmhouse I know, all the hall furniture is covered with a quite remarkable contemporary print, and there are lots of gay pictures all around. Another lovely living hall is filled with flowering plants all winter bathed in sunlight from French doors.

Even a tiny hall, lined with doors and scarcely large enough for a magazine and mail table, can be a wonderful little ornament for a house. In La Fiorentina in the South of France, there is just such a hall. Visitors hardly notice it as they enter, they're so overwhelmed by the enormous scale of the house. But on the way out, their eyes are caught by the wonderful trompe l'oeil murals of Grecian urns and gardens—a final surprise that never fails to delight.

The hallway, that rather narrow, often deadly little sliver of space that serves as a bridge between important rooms, is another place that needs thought and imagination to make it pleasant, let alone livable. Even though you never sit down in a hallway, it always seems sad to be prompted to hurry through.

If the living halls can sparkle with extra color and pattern, a little hallway can be a firecracker. Just the application of a terrific color can charge a drab hall with vitality. You stay there so briefly—why not make it a dazzling experience? Of course, in a hallway that is an extension of another room, I would not go so far as to introduce an altogether new and unrelated color. If the living room is done in shades of apricot, for instance, I might paint the hallway a rich, almost tomato color—intensi-

Spindles of glass support the blue banister in the entrance hall, opposite, just because they look pretty, and because my clients, Mr. and Mrs. James Fentress, wanted something the other side of ordinary. The little white room is full of doors, so we played them up by painting their moldings navy blue—a harbinger of the blue-and-whiteness of the rest of the house.

43

Overleaf: A very graphic room that belongs to Woodson Taulbee. The Matisse above the sofa inspired the printed cotton that covers all the upholstered furniture.

fication, rather than competition. Or I might wallpaper the hall with a brilliant pattern that would simply be too much for the living room. Although there's no need for any other ornamentation when you use wallpaper, don't make the mistake of thinking that it precludes hanging pictures. A hallway can make a wonderful little gallery for drawings, prints, and even small paintings that might be lost if the room were bigger. I would never hang a large painting in a narrow hallway, though. To really see it, you'd have to be pinned against the opposite wall.

Doors are inevitable in a hallway, so make the most of them—with mirror, brilliant-colored lacquer, or trompe l'oeil moldings and panels. Windows, on the other hand, are such a blessing that I leave them almost entirely alone. Shutters are all I add, a big potted plant in each window is even better.

When a hall is wide enough, it's nice to have some furniture, even if only a bench or the skinniest little console table. On that table I love to see a bowl of flowers, or a lamp that makes a soft light for guests in the night, haloing rather than illuminating the room. For serious lighting, the best kind is ceiling spots, shining down on the walls. Nothing is worse than a hallway where only the ceiling is lit—you feel as if you're groping your way through a tunnel.

The loveliest hallway I know is in a fantastic modern adobe house in Arizona. It is a rather long hall and tall, with three guest-room doors facing broad windows that overlook the patio and the pool. The walls are white, the floor is paved with pinky terra-cotta tiles, and all around hang wonderful contemporary pictures. For a guest in that house, it is the loveliest pleasure to step out in the morning to this beautiful sunlit room. And in the evening, you can sit in the patio and see, through the great curtainless windows, those remarkable paintings lighted by hanging lanterns. Far from being mere architectural necessity, that hallway is a beautiful jewel of a room that would make any house proud.

How to live
in your living room

I can hardly go into a house or an apartment today without finding a great big living room that consumes the most space in the house, is filled with the most expensive furniture, the best pictures, the most precious objects—and is almost never used. I've seen it happen time and time again: Visitors come in, look around, admire, then invariably walk on to another, smaller, more intimate room to sit in. Let's be honest about it. That big room isn't the living room at all. Unless you have a great many rooms, that is a ghastly waste of space. The living room should be lived in.

The first thing I do to make a living room livable is to furnish it with big soft sofas and upholstered chairs that just beg to be sat in. Lots of people fill their "showcase rooms" with museum-quality antique chairs, then glower at anyone who tries to sit on them. These people have a strange kind of reverence for anything that is old and expensive. I love to look at antique chairs. But I also like to sit on them. Have a few beautiful antique open armchairs in your living room if you want to, but make the backbone of the room deeply comfortable upholstered furniture.

Once I've assembled all this voluptuous furniture, I like to arrange it in small separate groups, like garden plots, so that when you settle down in one of them, the rest of the room becomes background. You can make the divisions even more distinct by using area rugs, rows of potted plants, folding screens, or freestanding bookcases.

It would be very clever to make each area a kind of activity group that the family would be drawn to naturally. Some of the furniture could be grouped around the piano, for instance. Another group, with a letter-writing table nearby, could face the fire. Still another might include the television, or walls lined with books, or a table and chairs for family games. Or, you might even designate one entire area for dining, guaranteeing the room will be used two or three times a day.

People don't seem to realize how pleasant it is to have dinner in the living room. After the main course, and just before dessert, you can clear the table and remove the cloth (unless you're so engrossed in the conversation that you forget), then serve the coffee, dessert, and after-dinner liqueurs right there. Guests can push comfortably away from the table and still have their drinks right at their fingertips. The conversation won't be disrupted by a move, yet you will be in a living-room ambience.

When you arrange your living-room furniture, think less of symmetry and more of comfort. Some rooms always look as if the decorator has just left—all the furniture is in a line, all the corners square. But when guests come and the conversations get lively, a marvelous thing happens: Chairs are turned around and pulled up to where they are really more comfortable (it's a good idea to have some pull-up chairs that can be moved around easily). And after everyone leaves, the room looks much better than it did at first. I don't mean you have to arrange all your furniture in a circle. But remember that if you put a tall lamp or vase of flowers on a table between two chairs, the people in those chairs won't be able to see each other.

When it comes to color, think warm. Deep vibrant colors like brown, red, or burnt orange make a room intimate without reducing its size. I like to see furniture covered with chintz in a traditional room, or with a wonderful contemporary pattern in a more modern room. I love to see objects around—not a clutter, as you'd have in a smaller room, but enough so everyone knows this room belongs to someone—things happen here. One of the nicest living rooms in New York belonged to one of my colleagues, Mrs. Henry Parish II, who knows just how to live in a living room. The walls were dark brown. The curtains were the color of coral, and there was a wonderful English garden chintz on all the big overstuffed chairs and sofas. She had arranged the furniture in three groups—one of them around the fire. Here was where she sat every day to have a cup of tea and read the mail. Here was where the family gathered, drawn by the firelight on chilly afternoons. The room was equally beautiful when filled with people or when you were alone there. That's what I call a room that's lived in.

CONTEMPORARY
AMERICAN
PAINTINGS
SET AGAINST
MATISSE COLORS

*W*hen Mr. and Mrs. Harding
Lawrence asked architect
*Page Cross and me to warm up
their gloomy Tudor house in Dal-
las, I saw almost at once that the
solution was going to be color. So
after Mr. Cross gutted and almost
entirely redesigned the interior, I
went in with the most cheerful
colors I know—the sunny palette
of Matisse paintings. When Mr.
Cross was through with it, the living room,* right and below, *became
a wonderful big square room, with
very nice windows, a high ceiling,
and a big fireplace—really the
perfect room to work with. I immediately decided on that pink
exactly the color of raspberry ice,
with pure white moldings and
ceiling. Sofas are covered with
white linen; chairs and ottomans
in a wonderful flowered glazed
chintz exactly—and on my honor,
coincidentally—the colors of the
huge painting by Stamos above the
sofa. The exciting thing about the
house is its pictures—almost all
of them contemporary American.
Modern white lacquer coffee tables
and an old black-lacquer corner
cupboard punctuate the room.*

A LIVING ROOM THAT'S AN OPEN-ARMS KIND OF ROOM

Mrs. Clive Runnells' Florida house is geared for comfort, fun, and coolness. Every fabric is cotton, the rugs are tough Moroccans, and shutters, perfect for Florida, take the place of curtains everywhere but in the bay window. All the furniture came from Mrs. Runnells' former Florida house except the two dashing Chinese hatboxes, which we put to use as end tables. Even the deep blue of the print is a repeat, although the pattern was changed (it used to be butterflies), because Mrs. Runnells finds deep blue cool, calming, and a nice color to have around. Her favorite treasures in the room are the porcelain foot warmers in the shelves behind the sofa.

Your bedroom—
the most personal room
in the house

Years ago I worked on a very fashionable and luxurious master-bedroom suite: for madame, a huge boudoir with bath and dressing room; and for monsieur, a monk's cell under the eaves. Today our ideas about comfort have changed. Aside from the rooms that look like gymnasiums for fear of being too feminine, most bedrooms are what they should be—another living room, more private, more romantic, more personal than the living room itself, and always extravagantly comfortable.

First of all, you should have the best mattress you can buy, roomy enough and long enough so you can sleep without dangling your feet over the edges like fringe. Have a bedside table on each side of the bed (not necessarily a pair—we've been freed from that irrational restriction), each with a drawer for tissues, pills, and other needs. By all means have a lamp on each side of the bed, too. My favorite is the swing-arm, wall-hung kind because it leaves the entire tabletop free for radio, clock, water carafe, your book, and maybe a pretty bunch of flowers. Or, if you like to read or do needlepoint while your husband sleeps, a little high-intensity spotlight won't disturb him and takes up almost no space.

Natural light is the villain in the morning. It can shatter otherwise sublime comfort into absolute irritation. If you wake at the first streak of morning light that cracks through the window, have the curtains lined and interlined in flannel and black sateen. And have them cut taller and wider than the window, with a generous overlap when they're drawn. If you must have fresh air as well as total darkness, you need practical curtains of cotton or duck rather than perishable silks. Line them with aluminum treated fabric, and, if they are light in color, interline them with white flannel.

Everything in a bedroom should contribute to an atmosphere of peace. For some, this means extreme neatness—just the necessities, with plenty of space between. Others make their bedrooms part sitting room and invite friends there for tea or drinks. One couple I know keep the living room for entertaining and do most of their living in the bedroom. Their living room is comfortable, of course, with lots of little bibelots and mementos that are very dear to them—but it is extremely orderly. Their bedroom is the complete antithesis. Books are piled everywhere, even on the floor beside the bed. A desk is cluttered with papers and unfinished business. You can tell that letters are actually written and bills actually paid there.

The bedroom ought to be the most personal room in the house, without regard to what may be promoted as "bedroom colors" or "bedroom styles." Some of the best city bedrooms I know have untraditional dark walls—peaceful gleaming chocolate brown, dark green, even black lacquer, with lots of printed cotton. In the country there is nothing as charming as a white bedroom with sprigs of color, fresh as a bouquet of flowers.

The most luxurious bedrooms have as little dressing equipment as possible. Building plans should always include a separate dressing area, with lots of drawer and closet space, and mirrors everywhere. If you own a house, you can often turn an adjoining bedroom into a dressing room and bath—I would do so even if it meant making the master bedroom a bit smaller. If a dressing room is impossible, there is, fortunately, unbedroomy looking furniture you can find if you search. A generous armoire, for instance, with shelves or hanging space and long mirrors concealed behind its doors is a beautiful substitute for the functional chest-of-drawers.

The chaise longue, which used to be an absolute requirement, doesn't seem to pull its weight anymore. You can nap so much more comfortably right on the bed. This also explains why pretty but practical blanket covers are often substituted for bedspreads. A more versatile seating idea would be an armchair and an ottoman that becomes a table for the Sunday paper or an extra seat without taking up the slightest bit more space. The dressing table is often replaced by the bathroom counter since so many women prefer to make up in the bathroom. There is one old-fashioned extravagance that is as important today as ever: the big, heroically scaled bed. I love bedrooms that look as if the bed takes up the whole place—old-fashioned beds with tall posts and canopies or curtains.

When you wake up in the morning, the first thing you see should be the most beautiful thing in the room—a window facing the sea or a garden. Or a serene painting. It will put you in a good frame of mind, so that when your husband awakens, the most beautiful thing in the room will be you.

PURE SHUT-OUT-THE-WORLD COMFORT

Comfort is the whole idea behind Mr. and Mrs. Thomas Kempner's bed-sitting room in New York. The walls are hung with soft, creamy muslin shirred on rods top and bottom and bordered with a striped French fabric we repeated on the bed and on the wall behind the bed. For a feeling of restfulness, there is an almost total absence of legs. Two tables are covered to the floor, one in flowers, one in a second stripe. In front of the fireplace across from the bed, a pair of tufted chairs and a swooping Victorianesque sofa are covered with a glazed Edwardian chintz patterned with double poppies—the flower of sleep. The door is an accent of blues: sapphire with turquoise panels, the moldings prettily picked out in white.

52

Whatever happened
to the
dining room?

Not so many years ago, the dining room was the ultimate in pomp and circumstance. In the center of every large dining room was an endlessly long table, where two dozen diners lined up shoulder to shoulder like New York town houses. You were expected to chat first with your neighbor on one side, then on the other. And if one of them failed to give you his attention, there you'd be, staring at your plate. Often what was on that plate was quite ordinary. As recently as five years back I went to two dinner parties on successive evenings at two different houses in Newport. Both parties were in rather large, formal dining rooms, and both dinners were entirely arranged by the same caterer. Menus and flowers were exactly alike. On the second evening, even the butler and waitresses gave you a smile of recognition. Fortunately some—but not all—of the guests were different, so I was sure the second party wasn't just a nightmare of the night before.

Today, thank goodness, we are more concerned with the personal in entertaining than with perfection. Dinner parties have shrunk in size, blossomed with variety in food and decoration, and spread out to every room in the house. For big parties, we have accepted that wonderful invention, the buffet, at which people get up from their chairs and move around, and conversation goes on all over the room. And more and more, the big long table is giving way to more versatile round ones.

The William Blair's house in Washington—one of those lovely old ones with a circular staircase in a center hall—has a drawing room to the left and what once was a very formal long dining room to the right. Today that dining room is largely a living room, with a big oyster-white sofa, a pair of Louis XVI armchairs covered with an interrupted pinstripe of green and white, and a large glass, bronze, and steel coffee table. Windows are curtained with unlined apple-green taffeta that looks just like lettuce leaves when the sun shines through them. The only clue that this might also be a dining room is a pretty round table near the fireplace, covered to the floor with

A roomful of books can make the simplest meal a pleasure. In Mrs. Munn Kellogg's pale, quiet dining room-library, white walls, broken only by the reseda-green silk curtains at the tall windows, are entirely lined with books, even above the doors. In the corner by one window is the round dining table, always covered to the floor with a pretty salmon-pink cloth. The painted Venetian chairs are part of a set of eight—the others, scattered around the room and the hall, are ready to be pulled up to a long table Mrs. Kellogg sets up when she has more than six for dinner. Also in the room: a sofa, deep comfortable chairs, excellent reading lights.

creamy French taffeta all sprigged with flowers in porcelain colors. Around it are four more green-striped chairs. When there are more than four dinner guests, a card table topped with a round of plywood is brought in and the two living-area chairs—plus another pair from the hall—provide luxuriously comfortable dining in a beautiful living-room atmosphere—or library as books line one wall!

In a house of similar plan in Baltimore, the walls between drawing room, hall, and dining room have been removed to form one gigantic room with two facing fireplaces. It has white walls, scarlet damask curtains, and lots of upholstered furniture. A large screen, made of a very old Aubusson rug too fragile for the floor, cuts off the far third of the room, and behind the screen, invisible from the front door, is the dining table. A much more sensible division of space.

One of my favorite combination dining rooms is the Paul Mellon's kitchen on Cape Cod. The walls are paved with blue and white Portuguese tiles, and all the counters are scrubbed butcher blocks. There is a big old stove with a shiny steel hood and a rack hung with marvelous pots and pans. Huge windows look out on a flower and vegetable garden, and glass doors opposite them lead to a terrace. The round dining table is always covered with a calico cloth and surrounded with white-painted Hitchcock chairs. And there is always a jug of wildflowers. During dinner, bowls of second helpings wait on a nearby countertop along with a pitcher of wild carrots or some other simple field flower. Of course you must be neat about your cooking to bring off a dinner in the kitchen—I wouldn't like very much to eat gazing at a sinkful of used pots and pans.

One house I know has no dining room whatever. The lady who lives there takes her meals wherever it is most pleasant—between two windows in the library, for instance, where there is a lovely backgammon table teamed with two upholstered armchairs. When there are two for lunch, on goes a tablecloth, and that space becomes the dining room. A handsome French writing table by the living-room fireplace can seat four on a blustery day. And, for those times when the sun strikes the bedroom window in a particularly lovely way, a table stands waiting there.

To be really pleasant for dining, a room must be relatively quiet—I mean the visual quiet of drawn curtains and soft light as well as the absence of clatter. An over-lit room is a horror for eating. The temperature of a dining room is also very important. A too-hot room can take away your appetite. Before every dinner party, no matter how cold the day. I think the door should be closed and the windows opened for at least half an hour—this, also, for the elimination of cooking smells.

When you decorate the tables, beware of centerpieces with too many flowers in too-big bouquets. Much more charming is a simple flowering plant in its own clay pot or a little wicker basket—and please don't have strongly scented flowers. I remember one dinner party in the tropics where the smell of the tuberoses on the table was enough to knock you down.

Above all, a dining room should be comfortable. The Calvin Fentress dining room in Lake Forest has clear-yellow walls and matching raw-silk curtains, the table is round, the Louis XVI upholstered chairs extraordinarily comfortable—four open armchairs, two fully upholstered bergères. You almost wish dinner would go on forever.

Checking out the guest room

Often, when I stay at a friend's house over-night or for the weekend, the hostess says to me, "I hope the room is comfortable." I suppose she thinks her words are a sweet benediction, but they fill me with anxiety. Because then I know she hasn't tried the guest room herself.

The guest room should be just as comfortable as your own bedroom, and the only way you can be sure of it is to move in yourself for a trial weekend. Then you'll notice that all the drawers are full of extra blankets or last year's Christmas decorations, or that the light bulb needs replacing, or that the most recent magazine in the room is dated 1958. If the guest is to be a man, have your husband perform the trial run. I can't tell you how often I find guest-room closets full of lovely tufted-satin hangers—and no way to hang a pair of trousers.

If two people are to share a room, I think you should provide them with sepa-rate reading lights, individually controlled, with beams that concentrate on the books. Chances are one will want to go to sleep just when the other is getting to the good part. I think each guest should have his own bedside table, too, uncluttered by little paperweights and bunches of flowers. It's so much nicer, anyway, to wake up in the morning and see the flowers on a table across the room. And a vacant bedside table to put your own things on is much more appreciated than paperweights. A hostess can provide a thermos of ice water and a glass, and in a drawer, tissues. If the table is small, the reading light can be hung above it on the wall. You can have a switch in-serted in the cord at a point easy to reach, even in the dark, by someone lying in bed.

The most unforgettable guest room I've slept in was so comfortable and thoughtfully arranged it looked as if it were occupied permanently. In a window, for instance, was a lovely writing table with a chair, so you could write letters by the morning light. On the table were pretty writing paper and very good pens—not worn-down pencils stuck carelessly in a drawer. On the end of a sofa was a wonderful afghan, and on tables, potted flowers that were changed every other day. I found a few new books, current magazines, and every morning, the paper. All of this at "Mouton" the chateau of the Baron and Baroness Philippe de Rothschild.

If there is a special bathroom for guests, that, too, should be carefully scrutinized before a guest arrives. One bathroom a friend of mine occupied had not a single hook anywhere to hang his robe on while he showered. Not accustomed to keeping silent about such inconveniences, the next morning at breakfast he asked his mortified hostess for a hook. Just as perplexing as no hook is a badly placed hook—stuck, for instance, above a mirror on a door. You've got to remove your pajamas so you can straighten your tie. Other guest-bathroom considerations: Is the light strong enough for shaving or making-up? Is there instant hot water in unlimited supply? Are there hand towels within easy reach of the washstand? Is there counter space or a table for guests' belongings, a hamper for used towels, a wastebasket impervious to such things as cotton soaked in nail-polish remover or creams? If the bathroom is large, it's lovely to have a slipper chair, which I very often cover in preshrunk turkish toweling bought by the yard. But be sure to have a duplicate slipcover made so one can always be fresh.

The medicine cabinet, too, should be as well-equipped as your own—plenty of Band-Aids, aspirin, antacid, extra toothbrushes and paste, bobby pins, shower caps, razor blades, tissues, hair spray and air spray, and a fresh bar of soap. Not only is it a great kindness to provide these for your guest, it also avoids unhappiness if he's too polite or too shy to ask for something he's forgotten—and your embarrassment if he makes a great performance of going down to Main Street to shop.

Housekeeping must go on throughout your guest's stay. If the chair cover shows the slightest sign of soil, it should be changed and laundered. Towels must be collected and a fresh supply installed. You should also check to see what has been used up, exchanging soap scraps and twisted toothpaste tubes for fresh plump ones. A no-maintenance touch: potted plants in place of a vase of flowers.

Naturally the guest must bear some of the responsibility for keeping the room attractive. I don't like things to look out of place anywhere, and I would never want anyone picking up after me just because I was away from home. You can be considerate, too, about your hosts' family life. For me breakfast is a cup of coffee and a slice of toast. If I can have them in my room while I write a letter or read the morning paper my day begins just right—and my host and hostess get another hour to themselves. Everyone, host and guest alike, welcomes privacy.

Let nature
help you decorate an
outdoor room

Recently I was the guest of a woman whose pride and joy was her tropical rooftop garden, a beautiful terraced roofscape of fruit trees, ferns, exotic flowers, and orchids. In this delightful setting, we had cocktails before a dinner party, and it would have been perfectly wonderful except for one thing. That night there was, not a breeze, but a gale wind. Women's hair whipped into their eyes. Hors d'oeuvres blew off tables and ashes out of ashtrays. Nerves were wracked, composures frazzled. Yet our hostess was oblivious. She was so in love with her rooftop paradise that she gave no thought whatsoever to its faults.

Summer's treasures are like uncut stones—to make them gems, you've got to do some polishing. That roof garden could have been protected by wind screens. For dinner on the terrace when the wind threatens to blow charcoal-cooking smells into your fruit-and-rum hors d'oeuvres, you can set up the party upwind. If everything fails, be wise enough to give up and go inside.

Much as everyone loves Old Sol, he can sometimes become overbearing. Always provide some shade, especially when you eat outdoors, as a buffer between the heat of the sun and cool serenity. Shade can be as simple as a covered porch or awninged terrace, or, on the lawn, a gazebo or vine-covered trellis, an umbrella, or even a big tree. In Maryland, where I grew up, we'd all have after-tennis mint juleps under a catalpa tree so sprawling it formed an actual room. In another part of Maryland, some clever people I knew formed an outdoor room with an octagon of clipped privet hedge that had an archway cut into one side and a tree for a roof. The beautiful garden of the Harold Christie's in Nassau is divided by the plantings into rooms—one for cocktails, one for after-dinner coffee—each with plenty of shade trees and lots of open sunshine. Another family I know planted an orange tree in the greenhouse they use as a summer room. It reaches to the glass ceiling, making wonderful, scented shade. All around the side walls are upside-down roll shades that pull upward along the slant of the glass. I found a most ingenious way to make shade in Jamaica, where a C-shaped house is built around an open pool. When the sun gets too strong, strips of canvas 36 inches wide can be pulled across one at a time from the roof of one wing to the other, forming a fabric ceiling over part or all of the pool area.

With every sunny day, you get its troublesome by-product—glare. How often have you stood on a beautiful terrace looking out to sea and been blinded by the glare? Or, when sitting opposite someone lucky enough to have the sun behind him, found you were talking to a dark silhouette? I once decorated a loggia for Mrs. Gilbert Miller in Mallorca, where traditional Mediterranean draw curtains failed to eliminate the problem—they gave us total darkness. We finally hit on the idea of Roman shades—the same as you might use in a living room—that can be lowered as you need them. They cut the upper glare without cutting out light entirely or separating people in the shade from people in the sun. They can be made almost limitlessly wide or can be divided into sections for more flexible light control. One Mediterranean tradition that does help to cut glare: painting the porch ceiling blue or sea green rather than white. The difference it makes is amazing.

A summer night outdoors, unless there is a brilliant moon, brings its own lighting problems—bright spots in your eyes, or no light at all so that everyone sits in total darkness, uncomfortably talking to disembodied voices and the ends of glowing cigarettes. Although there are some beautiful electric fixtures designed for outdoors, candles are still my favorite summer lights. On a dining terrace or outdoor sitting area, I would have them all around the edges, always in hurricane globes, plus a few on the table for sparkle.

No one who has given it any thought ever claimed that the upkeep of an outdoor room is less work than one inside. People sometimes have an it-doesn't-matter-because-it's-only-outdoors attitude. But the reason you are outdoors in the first place is to enjoy the cleanness, the freshness. If you let the chairs rust and the cushions mildew, you destroy that pleasure. Make sure ashtrays are deep enough to keep the ashes inside. Use plates and glasses heavy enough so they won't be blown away. Why not vinyl covers on everything—and a box or closet to keep them in during sudden squalls, overnight, and whenever you're away? I sometimes suggest building a banquette with a flip-up seat for the cushions, or a big padlocked box, painted to match the furniture. If your outdoor room has latchable shutters, it forms its own box.

While we often speak of bringing the look of the outdoors in, it turns out to be more of a problem to keep the real outdoors out, especially if there's a beach or a swimming pool nearby. No hostess likes to follow her guests around, mopping behind them. Most guests will respect your house and do everything they can to preserve its contents. It's up to you to provide the means. If you're planning a new house, a very good idea is a mud room or a dressing room for swimmers with a cabinet full of towels, hooks for clean clothing, and perhaps an adjoining bath with a shower. In an older house, you may have to improvise. In one house I know, the hostess rolls strips of heavy awning canvas that match the carpeting over the most heavily trafficked areas. In another house, where the painted floors are smooth as cream, there are good-sized woven mats at every doorway. In still another, the most inspired idea of all: in every first-floor bath, not a window, but an outside door. Even if you can't be that elaborate, you can at least provide a faucet, a bucket, and a towel.

Lots of people think sports equipment is untidy looking and worry about where to put the inevitable badminton birdies that appear with summer flowers. I don't think the paraphernalia that is so much a part of summer life should be hidden at all. Think of those charming English halls, the long bench stacked with tennis rackets and boxes of balls, a golf bag leaning nearby. The fun is part of the decoration.

Some things belong uniquely to summer. The smell of boxwood is to me the essence of a summer day—no one in Maryland was without at least one box bush, and that fragrance, brought out by the heat of the sun, seemed to permeate the whole world. At night, there are all kinds of beautiful perfumes, yours for the planting: honeysuckle, orange trees, heliotrope, nicotiana, white petunias. And there are the summer sounds—crickets, rustling trees with hidden windbells tinkling in their branches, the roar of the ocean or the splash of a stream or a fountain in the garden. In Mrs. Paul Mellon's Antigua house, there is a slat house adjoining the dining room where she kept, along with her orchids and seedlings, three tree toads that serenaded us all evening long. Let nature help you decorate an outdoor room: Hang baskets of ferns in an apple tree. Let the back lawn grow tall and meadowy. Invite ducks to the pond or a family of sparrows to a whimsical ante-bellum birdhouse. Then, in the middle of it all, nature will work her own miracle of the "lightning bugs," the most magical lighting in the world.

How to bring your rooms up to date

Often a client of long standing will ask me to come have a look at his house or apartment. Maybe he's had it the same way for a few years and thinks it needs a fresh look. Or perhaps a new fabric or wallpaper he's seen in a magazine has caught his fancy, and suddenly his own rooms seem drab. Sometimes he will hear of nothing short of a complete overhaul. But more often, if the rooms were beautiful to start with, just a few changes or additions will completely refresh them.

If the room is traditional, the key to bringing it up to date is to simplify. You might replace a butler's-tray coffee table, for instance, with one of clear or bronze translucent plastic—or with a sleek Parsons table in clear lacquer, red or yellow. Remove a few traditional side chairs or lamp tables and replace them with clean contemporary ones. In designing contemporary rooms, the accepted formula is to add an antique or two. What's wrong with the reverse?

Even the smallest details, like cigarette boxes and ashtrays, can make a room look old fashioned. Replace the dreary ones with Japanese lacquer (put rounds of glass in the bottoms of ashtrays to keep from burning) or with faceted glass.

Take stock of your lamps and lampshades. Fashions in lampshades change as rapidly and radically as the fashion in skirt lengths. More than anything else in the world, an old-fashioned lamp can put a room in the dark ages. Recently I saw a room full of colossal table-to-ceiling lamps, bases much too big, shades ridiculously over-scaled. They made the whole room look vulgar. Why not replace such lamps with honest contemporary ones? Or simplify the shades? The lampshades that give the best light, I think, and the smartest looking besides, are the ones of off-white paper, either opaque or translucent. Most rooms have too many lamps, and far too many shades. Take out some lamps, increase the wattage in others, and suddenly the whole room looks young and fresh.

Review your curtains. Sometimes all you have to do to bring a room up to date is to remove the valances. Replace heavy silks with clean fresh cottons. Or, if your windows are beautiful and the views are worth looking at, replace the curtains with louvered shutters or simple blinds.

The wallpaper, too, might be out-of-dating the room. If the paper is crowded with pattern and not very remarkable, you might want to remove it and paint the wall instead. If it's very good wallpaper, antique perhaps, you can take another simplifying tack: Add a few pieces of simple upholstered furniture, all covered with fresh, uncluttered cotton.

If you're a compulsive collector, tabletops fill quickly. When you find a table cluttered with lots of old-fashioned ornaments you're no longer particularly fond of, put them away or arrange them in some other room for a while, and leave the table shining. Or replace them with one beautiful piece of sculpture for instant vitality.

The same is true for contemporary paintings. Unless you're really in love with your old pictures, experiment with modern paintings and those wonderful modern drawings. Most galleries will let you try them before you decide to buy, and they put the whole room in a new light.

Freshening a contemporary room is a somewhat different problem, for contemporary rooms are by definition "up to date." Still, after four or five years, many clients begin to want a change. In that case, try adding antiques—especially timeless Chinese antiques. Or get a couple of antique sidechairs out of storage if you have them (don't buy new ones unless they're really good antiques, and you really love them), and recover them to go with the room. Or just put in one simple chair of natural or white wicker. If the room needs more change, a switch in slipcovers might be the refresher. But save the old ones to put back next year. I've alternated slipcovers in my own apartment for many years, and every change seems to make the room look new again.

Whatever changes you decide on to perk up a room, try to avoid change merely for the sake of change. To add something new—especially an expensive something—just because it's fashionable, is a poor investment and poor judgment besides. Stick to the things you really love. An honest room is always up to date.

LIVING WITH FLING
IN SMALL QUARTERS

So charged with the owners' personalities are some memorable rooms that it takes time to become aware that often they started with skimped space. Here and on the next four pages are three small rooms in three small New York apartments—one of them my own. At least two of these rooms are ungainly in shape; none has proportions worth praising. In each, we simply erased dimensions as a matter of concern. Most noticeable about these rooms are their differences. And then the similarity of palette—a similarity almost, but not quite, coincidental. A kind of intuition causes people at the same time, unwittingly, to want the same effect. The success of these rooms depends, in part, on respect and enthusiasm for other people's tastes—small treasures, fond furniture, odd pillows, favorite pictures. The idea is to make a little seem, effortlessly, a lot.

Almost too tall for its own good, Woodson Taulbee's "Tall Room" needed to have its height exaggerated, as if that's how we intended it to look all along. To lead the eye upward, we hung a beautiful black-iron Spanish chandelier, and left the tall narrow windows curtainless. All the rest of the furniture is low and wall-hugging (except for a wonderful French chair in the center), which also serves to keep the room uncluttered. Above the sofa hangs a brush and ink by Matisse—the inspiration for the coffee-brown and white cotton that covers all the upholstered furniture.

A TALL ROOM,
CLEAN AND
UNCLUTTERED

14' 6"

15'

AREA A

AREA B

The focus for entertaining is the corner banquette (right, area B), *a good way to get a lot of people in a little space. In the sitting area* (left, area A), *the lacquer of tables and a Chinese screen glisten, while brown suede, fur, and velvet give a depth.*

*E*ssentially a library I sleep in, my own one-room apartment is a low-ceilinged, awkwardly shaped affair with all the usual juts and protuberances of modern apartment buildings. First I x'ed out beams and bumps with a coat of shiny dark-brown paint. Then I grouped the furniture according to purpose: Area A, *left, became the bedroom, with a pillow-piled sofa that is really a standard twin bed in disguise. Area B, above, is for sitting. And area C, below right, consists of a writing table in front of the windows.*

It occurred to me that this was strictly a city room, full of shine: the floor, the walls, the windows. So I added more shine: a varnishy eighteenth-century painting of dogs, a wonderful Korean lacquer screen, and a few strategically placed mirrors. I put all my books on tall brass bookshelves—the warm glint of brass became terribly important to the dark room. For comfort and softness, the rugs are fur, the upholstered furniture all very smooth and plump. I have three sets of slipcovers: blue denim, dark paisley, ivory cotton.

THE LOOK
OF A LIBRARY
FOR ONE-ROOM LIVING

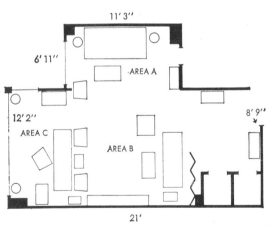

11' 3''

6' 11''

·AREA A

12' 2''

AREA C

AREA B

8' 9''

21'

A CURTAINED ROOM FOR A COLLECTOR

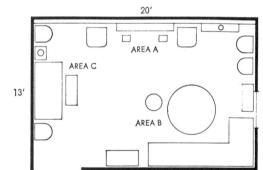

*T*o create a background for a really beautiful collection of objects became the challenge of Speed Lamkin's small living room. To do it, we hung the walls nonstop in shirred curtains of printed cotton, pulled back to show sudden vistas of window, mirror, bookshelves, or door. A big corner banquette is covered in the same fabric. The effect is an almost dizzying absence of dimension. To compound the feeling, we added lots of extra pattern: paisley pillows that interrupt the banquette's print; two French cut-velvet chairs flanking a mottled marble mantel, old paintings of animals on mirrors that multiply the pattern all around. The room is Mr. Lamkin's favorite for entertaining. Dinner for six is served at a round table pushed up to the banquette (above, area B). He usually sets tea on the low lacquered table by the sofa (below left, area C), *and thirty people for cocktails simply fill the open room.*

Nothing is in good taste
unless it suits
the way you live.
What's practical
is beautiful...
and suitability always
overrules fashion.

3

HOW TO WORK WITH A DECORATOR

You
and your decorator's
trained eye

If you have marvelous taste and know exactly what you want, you don't need a decorator. Some of the prettiest rooms I've seen have been done by one woman all by herself. But it's very difficult for most people to do things for themselves. There are so many beautiful things today that to strain out all but what's best for you is a real job. A decorator's job.

You should only go to a decorator whose work you have seen and believe in. You might be tempted to approach someone with a fashionable name. But if his taste doesn't match up with yours, his name won't make up for it. You must also like each other. I know some decorators who say they'd like to murder their clients, and I suspect some clients feel the same way about their decorators. I don't know how you can create harmony out of such violent discord. Of course there will be times when you disagree. But if you begin with mutual respect, you will not be afraid to be frank.

When I think something is exactly right, I gather all my forces to explain why. If you disagree, you should be equally firm and rational. Getting all emotional never solves anything. Neither does being too pliable. Some people let their decorators do things they don't really like. Then later they say, "I just hate that sofa, but my decorator made me get it." That is as lame as saying, "They made me get drunk last night at the party."

There's no reason to feel embarrassed about not liking something. Your decorator must learn what you don't like as well as what you do. I think it's adorable when a woman says, "I am about to break your heart. I've tried my best, and I know you're right, but I just don't like that fabric. If you want to dump me, go ahead." Then I say, "Well I am disappointed, but it's not my chair, it's yours. If I can't come up with a fabric we both like, there is something the matter with me." If what is second best for me will make her happy, that's really better than perfection. There are times when I've said, "I believe so strongly that the chair should be covered with this fabric that

74

Overleaf: Detail from small library foyer at La Fiorentina, the Harding Lawrences' villa in the South of France.

If you were out all day and knew I was waiting at home in some silky dressing gown, what kind of mood would you be in? Do not expect your interest in me to be quenched by a lot of cold high-fashion atmosphere...

Do you realize that you're terribly sensual?

Do you realize that it matters very much how a chair feels when you sit in it? Do you realize that you're extravagantly crazy about luxury?

I'm going to do it anyway. Then if you still don't like it I'll do it over again for nothing." Often clients have fallen in love with the result, and sometimes I've had to say, "You were right—it's awful."

If you and I agree to work together, the first thing I do is try to learn everything there is to know about you—the way you and your family live, what kind of entertaining you do, which rooms the children use, the size and approximate muddiness of the dog's feet. You ought to bring up every question, every requirement, every idea you can think of. You should specify your budget without hesitating. I have an obligation to keep within that budget and still produce the most charming room I can conceive. A small budget never meant less style.

I think it's criminal to show a client something she can't afford. There is only one exception: if I find something so right and so beautiful that it would really make the whole room. Once I found a superb French writing table, and I told my client: "I know it would have to be over and above the budget, but what would you think of buying this instead of, say, a new fur coat?" Then it was up to her to decide whether or not the table was worth it to her.

I like to discuss all the basics face-to-face with my client, in her house, so I can get the feel of the rooms and her way of life. But there was one unique instance when I saw my clients only briefly, and never in their house. They were busy with work in another part of the country. So the wife wrote me letters—wonderful letters that described not how she wanted things to look, but how she wanted things to feel. For instance: "If you'd been out all day and knew I was waiting at home in some silky dressing gown, what kind of mood would you be in? Do not expect your interest in me to be quenched by a lot of cold high-fashion atmosphere. . . . Do you realize that you're terribly sensual? Do you realize that it matters very much how a chair feels when you sit in it? Do you realize that you're extravagantly crazy about luxury?" She was writing to me, you see, but she was talking to her husband. I got the whole picture immediately. We had the rapport a decorator expects to find once in a lifetime.

When a picture of what the room should look like begins to form in my mind, I draw a floor plan. Some clients get impatient. "We want to see some materials," they say. I love to see that kind of enthusiasm, but it's really much wiser to lay the groundwork first. The floor plan is the garden soil of a room, fertilized and cultivated. The decoration is the flowers.

I never like to do more than one furniture scheme. The most successful rooms I know have been done very quickly. With a flash of intuition the client says, "Yes, that's just right." Minor changes can always be made later, but the point of view is there. Indecision is a terrible enemy. I agree with Franco Zefferelli, who says he has learned he likes his original ideas better than his later ones. Indecision exhausts everyone. The client becomes bogged in confusion, I can't possibly sustain my interest, the fine creative thread is snapped, and the room is stillborn.

Once the basic plan has been worked out, we can begin with fabrics and color and details—the fun part. I show you things you wouldn't otherwise be able to find.

But I edit them first, wading through all the thousands of fabrics and colors to pick out the best three or four. I think it's wrong for a decorator to take a client to a wholesale fabric house. If you like blue and green, he should get you all the best blues and greens. One trip to a wholesale house will only start you thinking maybe you should have some red.

By this time we have become a working team. If I see a wonderful little table, I go right to the telephone and tell you about it. Or you might call me from an antique shop to ask what I think of a lamp you have found. Or we'll go together to look at dining chairs, and on the way talk about what it might be fun to do with the fireplace niches.

One evening, when I was at a party at a client's house, I heard someone ask her, "Whose idea was it to have that marvelous needlepoint rug?" My client looked at me and we both laughed—because we honestly could not remember. That's the ideal kind of relationship to have. Some people say a decorator is an artist. I suppose they're right in a way. But he doesn't create some kind of walk-in sculpture, he creates the atmosphere. And that cannot be done without you.

Why you need a decorator before you build

If you are planning to build a house—and you want it to be designed perfectly from foundation to rooftop for the way you live —you should make friends with two people right off the bat. One is your architect. The other is your decorator.

Not many people realize how important a decorator is even in the earliest stages of planning a house. Today, so many structural details affect the decorating of a house —often are a major part of it. I have found that some architects and clients plan houses from the outside in, concerning themselves far more with the pitch of the roof and shape of the windows than with what goes on inside. What looks beautiful from the road may be absolutely impossible to live in.

Even before you hire an architect, while you are still in the throes of deciding what kind of house you want—contemporary or traditional, tall or sprawling—take notice of the kinds of rooms you feel most comfortable in. If you find one that you think is in marvelous proportion, write down the dimensions, the height of the ceiling, the number of windows. Then the architect will have a concrete idea of what you like, and you'll never have to complain that "it's so much smaller than I expected," or "the ceiling is so low." I hear these laments too often—and too late.

After the plans are drawn and you are asked to approve them, you should sit down with your architect and decorator and ask a lot of picky questions.

Will doors crash into the furniture or compete with each other for swinging space? Do some thinking about doors. You may feel the same as a woman I know who begins to fidget after sitting in a room for two minutes unless all the doors are closed. "Open doorways make your eyes wander out of the room," she says. "If there is the slightest amount of movement at the door, it snaps your concentration, rattles the peace, and interrupts your conversation." Doors that are kept closed most of the time should be more decorative, perhaps, or completely camouflaged so they blend with the wall.

Look for the light switches. Will you be able to light every room before you enter it? Are there enough wall sockets? I think wall sockets should be everywhere, sometimes even in the middle of the floor so you can have lamps there without snaking wires under the rug. Putting in lots of sockets as the house is being built costs almost nothing. Having a single one installed later can cost plenty. Have you thought enough about lighting fixtures? Some must be built into the house—spotlights for paintings and sculpture, lighting for objects in bookshelves, lights in the floor, outdoor lighting for the garden. It's very important that the architect and decorator work out the lighting in great detail, perhaps even calling in a third professional—the lighting expert—to be sure it is all perfect the first time.

The reason you must be so picayune is that reading a blueprint is so often misleading—you can hardly ever picture what the room will actually look like. One of the first things I look for in a blueprint is whether there is enough wall space for the furniture you will need. I was looking over some plans one afternoon, and there they were—all those huge windows again, taking up the whole master bedroom. "Will you kindly tell me," I asked in exasperation, "where I am expected to put the bed?" The architect, smiling, said, "Mr. Baldwin, those windows begin exactly thirteen feet from the floor." I was speechless. He handed me the elevation blueprint, and I could see then that the bedroom was just like a tower, with the whole top of glass. It was incredibly beautiful.

Elevations are as important as the floor plans and must be read as carefully. So often after the house is done, you find an awkward window or even discover you don't like one whole side of the house. Then you hear the terrible phrase: "Don't worry, we can plant it out." Will someone please explain why you should spend vast amounts to build the house of your dreams and then plant it out? How much more logical—and less costly—to take more time in the initial planning.

Recently, I was asked to decorate a kind of auditorium in the South. I was so impressed by what the architect had done that I decided to ask him how he thought the interior should be attacked. But when he began to talk about colors, I was aghast. "Those colors will destroy the lines," I said, "the incredibly beautiful flow that you want." I'll never understand how he could have created such a masterpiece without being able to follow it through. I suppose that's just the kind of thing that makes one man an architect and another a decorator—and makes you need them both to build the perfect house.

LA FIORENTINA,
A VILLA
FOR ACTIVE AMERICANS

Never in my long career have I seen two people so instantly conquered by a house as were Mr. and Mrs. Harding Lawrence, two quick, bright, fast-living Americans, when they first saw La Fiorentina. Before they even stepped inside the enchanting villa on the French Riviera, with its cloistered garden and grassy terraces that fall away to the sea, they knew they were destined to own it. They saw in the house a beautiful romantic resting place where they could go whenever they felt like forgetting their enormously busy work schedules for a while. "Let's have lots of linen and cottons, big puffy sofas and chairs, and good lights to read by," they said when I agreed to decorate the villa. "But let us remember that we bought the house because of what it is. Let's not revolutionize it." If the Lawrences were at first the captives of La Fiorentina, it now belongs utterly to them. When they first visited the villa, it was owned by Roderick Cameron, a travel writer and long-time friend of mine, and his mother, Lady Kenmare. They bought it in 1939 after the German High Command, who used it during the war, left it in utter ruins. Mr. Cameron completely redesigned the old house (nothing of the original stands today except the foundation and the cloister) and filled it with splendid furniture and Italian bronzes, all against a neutral background. The Lawrences were so enchanted by it that we decided only to simplify all the elegance for their modern

*Y*ou almost feel as if you're walking on a bridge, so airy and full of light is the living room, right, an enormously tall dazzling room that forms the cross-piece of the H-shaped house. Poised between a garden and the sea, the living room is furnished for peace and comfort: islands of soft padded sofas and chairs—all washed in tranquil blue. On its seaward side, tall French doors lead to a terrace, above, then on down to the swimming pool and the sea. To inland, arched windows open on the cloistered garden. From the entrance court, left, the villa is entirely hidden, except for its portico copied from Palladio's Villa Rotunda in Vicenza, by orange trees with whitewashed trunks. The whitewash is supposed to keep bugs from dining on the fruit, but it also makes marvelous decoration.

American style of living, and to fill it with the contemporary American paintings and drawings they love. Before, the house was literally without color, like a photograph in black and white. We have simply reshot it in color. What I love most about the house—especially the living room—is its wonderful luminosity. By day, light from the garden streams through the arched windows to play with light from the windows facing the sea. At night, an ingenious lighting plan, by Charles Sevigny, a brilliant young American designer who lives in Paris, of ceiling spots and lamps on tables, sculptures the room with light and shadow into a space full of mystery and life. Upstairs, the house is like a series of personal spas, entirely devoted to the comfort of the Lawrences and their guests. There are two master bedrooms, one for summer and one, warmed by the distant southern sun, for winter. In the summer bedroom, the walls are covered with an old beige Chinese wallpaper with a design of white bamboo and little white birds with brilliant plumage that Lady Kenmare herself painted. The winter bedroom, except for lemon-yellow curtains, is entirely white: cool white-painted tile floor, bed hung with white cotton voile.

There are five guest rooms, each of them treated, as all guest rooms should be, like another master bedroom: comfortable, convenient, and full of personal luxuries. Every one of them is equipped with splendid reading lights, big comfortable armchairs to sit in, and smaller slipper chairs to throw things on. There is always a writing table with a mirror above that can just as easily be used as a dressing table. Most luxurious of all, each bathroom has a tall window placed so that when you relax in the bathtub you can gaze out across the sea.

Off the second-floor hall that leads to these bedrooms is a small alcove with a floor of worn old tiles manufactured in the South of France—not far, in fact, from the villa. The paintings are modern, the furniture stands entirely on its own. To me, this alcove symbolizes the entire house in microcosm: There's a deep respect for good design whether it be of man or nature, old or new, indigenous or imported. It's all a part of the young vibrant American lifestyle the Lawrences have brought to La Fiorentina. And La Fiorentina, with reason, is absolutely delighted.

Pattern in small doses, calmer than in an allover smash, creates a living room with a sense of serenity, yet is just plentiful enough to give the room life. Clear, fresh blue covers the upholstered sofas and chairs, a deeper blue checkerboards with white on the French woven rugs, and every blue imaginable mingles in the Indian handkerchief pillows. All over the room are masses of blue and white Chinese porcelains. The big lacquered coffee table was designed, as was much of the furniture spotted here and there, by Charles Sevigny.

*T*he glory of the living room is space and light, all emanating from the tall, broad French doors, left, *that take up practically two entire walls. One step beyond the inland doors and you are in the garden,* below left, *a chessboard of green dwarf privet and gray santolina set off by paths of ancient brick, and all enclosed by a tall cloister with openings arched like the living-room windows. At one end of the living room, through great faux-bois double doors,* near right above, *and past a dramatic painting by Stamos, is the entrance hall, with its charming surprise of trompe l'oeil Greek vignettes spotted around the walls. At the other end of the living room, flanking a lovely little stair hall, are Mr. Lawrence's study,* near right bottom, *and the library,* far right bottom, *with its own small foyer,* far right top. *The library is used during the chilly winter months as a sitting room and during the summer as a kind of retreat from a houseful of guests. To make the room cool as well as cozy, the colors were kept pale and fresh, the patterns open and precise. The boiserie is glazed the color of straw, with matching curtains of crisp linen. The furniture is covered with green and yellow flowers, the rug with green and yellow checks. On the fireplace wall, a series of collages by Anne Ryan. In the library's little foyer hangs a huge white painting by Thomas Stokes. Mr. Lawrence's study across the hall is somewhat smaller than the library, but very tall, very masculine, and very comfortable. The walls and linen curtains are the color of hot biscuits, soft and warm like the glowing old marble floor. There are two Sheraton chairs, covered in leather exactly the color of English riding boots, and fat pillows made from Indian saris. On the walls, three nineteenth-century Persian paintings, the villa's only exceptions to a wonderfully varied collection of all-American art.*

A beautiful fresco, eighteenth-century Italian trompe l'oeil transferred to canvas—like a verdure tapestry in wonderful soft beiges and greens—covers the walls of the dining room, right, a charming, almost square room with a tranquil view of the sea. Three round tables for four are always covered to the floor with linen the rich color of earth. For dinner, floaty cloths of pretty pinky-beige linen are spread on top. In a little second-floor alcove, left, an eighteenth-century English lacquer desk faces a low yellow table taken from a design by Jean Michel Frank. Above each, a drawing by Jack Youngerman. On the rear wall hangs a painting by Cleve Gray.

The Lawrences spend most of their time at La Fiorentina on the terrace, near right, which in all but the dreariest weather serves as sitting room, dining room, and even party room. Simply furnished in natural wicker, white sailcloth, and potted lemon trees, the main terrace overlooks a series of grassy ones, densely bordered with mimosa, olive, cypress, and ancient pines. On the bottom-most terrace, just a splash from the Mediterranean, is the turquoise pool, below left, where lunch is sometimes served in the little apricot and white pavilion.

Suitability
is the quality
that makes things durable.
Be faithful to
your own taste because
nothing you really like
is ever out of style.

4
THE ELEMENTS OF DECORATION

The power
of color

A client of mine recently wanted to change her off-white dining room to something more exciting, but she had just inherited some Chippendale chairs and was afraid they would force her to have a forever-pale conventional room. She was so desperate that she was actually ready to sell the antiques. I told her that was the worst idea I had ever heard. Then I proceeded to do something I rarely do—I made a pair of watercolors of her dining room. The first was of the room as it was—walls, woodwork, rug, curtains, all off-white. In the second, I filled in the walls only with a raspberry sherbet wash. Even on paper the difference was unbelievable. After we repainted the actual room, we added a multicolor Bessarabian rug. I touched nothing else. This is the power of color. It gives a new life to old surroundings, and is the best thing for a budget because no one color ever costs more than another color.

Our current freethinking about color was really started years ago by the post-impressionist painters, who mixed unheard-of colors and used them in then shocking combinations like red and pink, blue and green. Even before that, the Victorians had a burning love for color, if not quite as fresh as today. The great silks of England and France and Italy were riotous and bold. Look on the wrong side of eighteenth-century embroidery and needlepoint, and you see it as it really was. The colors on the used side have been dimmed by time, sometimes into oblivion. For a while—not too long ago —people made a point of trying to conjure up antiquity by making everything in the room pallid and colorless like the used side of old needlepoint. Today we don't believe in starting out half dead.

The real danger now is that we may tend to go overboard with hard color. If you paint a wall a brilliant green, for instance, you have set the pace for the entire room. If you buy a high-colored and patterned antique rug—as much an investment as decoration—you'd better be sure you really like it. If you're less than sure, it's a

Surrounded by radiant color, the Mortimer Hall family really lives in the library. We put red velvet all over the walls, but brought it straight down to earth with the country print that covers all the upholstered furniture. The result is that the velvet relaxes—and everyone in the room relaxes, too. The windows are shuttered in tiers for perfect light control; alternating with them, fantastic tall mirrors for sparkle. In front of the window, a beautiful pierced Regency game table and lacquered chairs.

Overleaf: Seating around the fireplace in the Frederick Guests' country house.

93

better idea to keep the color in slipcovers and curtains. It doesn't involve much to switch from a green slipcover to a red one. You are also more likely to tire of a riotous pattern than of a more controlled one. There are remarkable exceptions, of course—rooms where each chair, picture, and object imposes its own personality, making it an extension of the owner's sure strong taste. But if a decorator tries to superimpose that kind of boldness, you won't be happy in the room for very long. By the same token, you'll tire of a color you've chosen only because you think it's fashionable. I hate to hear someone plead, "I know orange is in now, but I just love red. Can't I please have red?" Of course she can. No color you like is ever out of style.

During my experience as a decorator, I have developed a few rules of thumb about color: For walls, I find that strong colors or dark colors are best in shiny paint—what decorators call "lacquer." In my own apartment, the walls are very dark shiny brown. Picture that same color in a matte finish, and you would feel you were in the middle of a fallen chocolate soufflé. My office walls are also shiny, but white—a color that goes well in any finish. Of course shiny walls do bring up imperfections in the plaster, but if you break them up with a group of pictures or a tall piece of furniture, they can't be traced very far. And the shine gives the room so much more vitality. Soft colors and pastels, on the other hand, look best in flat paint—too much gloss on a pale-pink or pale-yellow wall makes it all shine, no color at all.

But you can glaze almost any darker color over a base color, giving a strié effect of three or four different tones. No matter what color the walls are, I nearly always like to make the woodwork and ceilings off-white. (There is something about colored mantelpieces that I can't abide.) What I often do is use pure white with just a drop of the wall color to soften it.

Most of us have gotten away, thank goodness, from classifying color by room. There are no "bedroom colors" anymore. I think a woman should ask only two questions about a color for her bedroom: "Do I like it?" and "Do I look well in it?" Yet lots of people still arbitrarily keep their bedrooms all pastels and sweetness. What's wrong with having a wonderful forest-green bedroom with lots of blue, or a white-lacquer library for a change?

One of my favorite color schemes is almost no color at all—those beautiful rooms of brown and beige and black and white, where the only vivid color is in the paintings and the varied tones of the books. These rooms usually need better furniture, however, simply because there is no brilliant color to make up for less-than-perfect tables and chairs. In a no-color room in a house in Spain, we put in a tall antique desk—a beautiful thing in scarlet lacquer so glowing that it made the whole room. Fabrics, too, must be better quality, or at least more textured than for color-

Magenta silks and the shimmer of mirror fill Mrs. Mollie Parnis Livingston's living room, which we created especially for her gala parties. Walls are white with the faintest blush of pink. Tall smocked curtains are soft magenta, a color repeated in stripes and patterns for a little slipper chair, a North African silk-covered ottoman, and a Louis XVI sofa and chairs. Over the sofa is a fantastic Picasso. Reflected in one of the mirrored panels between the windows, you can see a white marble mantel and, above it, a pair of antique gilt brackets holding amusing old Chinese porcelain roosters.

filled rooms. Cotton velvet, which I use all the time, looks more beautiful in deep jewel tones than in pastels.

If you have a collection of paintings, you may find they look more united against a background of color than against modern gallery white. When you furnish and color a room solely out of respect for a painting, you may be just venerating it and not making it a real part of your room.

Once you decide on the colors you want, look at every swatch of fabric, every color chip in the room's own light. Color is 100 percent affected by light. The other day I checked some fabrics for a city apartment, and they were fine in daylight. So I said, "Now we'll put them away until dark, when we won't have the benefit of outside light. If they are all right then, we'll use them." When you're trying to match colors it is absolutely essential to have the light they will mostly be seen in. Because of the different dye mixtures in different materials, colors that match in the decorator's office may not be happy in the lighting in your living room.

But I find I am more concerned with seeing the colors harmonize than with making sure they match. I sometimes wonder why so many decorators sit in wholesale houses leafing through swatch after swatch trying to find a precise match. I'd much prefer some other color—a variation on one of the colors in a print, for instance, or a blend of two colors. If you are timid about trying anything so daring as a nonmatching color, just think for a moment of a summer garden against the sky. Not one of the colors matches any other, and yet, can you think of anything more soul-satisfying?

The magic of materials and texture

The hardest thing about picking out just the right materials for your rooms is making up your mind. The variety is overwhelming. You can literally build a room with fabric alone. The difficulty is in knowing what to choose, and why.

My all-time favorite, as everyone knows by now, is cotton. It has such life, freshness, and variety in itself that you often need nothing else. There are marvelous den-

Texture and shine are doubly important in a no-color room like this former living room of mine. It was a small room, only 12 by 18 feet, but I still think it had great style. The keynote was lacquer: crackled black on the Portuguese table, gilt on a seventeenth-century Japanese cachepot, black and gold on that marvelous Korean screen. With it, a brown leather-covered chair I still can't part with, a patterned rug, and all manner of clutter—gifts from good friends.

ims, chintzes, polished cottons, sheers, cotton eyelets, corduroys, suede cloths, cotton velvets, wonderful thick handwoven cottons, and a cascade of tightweave silkscreened goods tumbling all over themselves in head-spinning profusion. Cotton goes with everything, modern furniture or antiques, gilt or wicker, and most other kinds of fabrics and materials, too. In an all-cotton room, you could easily cover a pillow or the seat of a small chair in silk damask or a bit of old tapestry without having it look the slightest bit out of place. If the room is to be very luxurious or if there is very good furniture or if you want a slightly formal atmosphere, you might also have curtains of silk (I mean silk with a handwoven look or perhaps dull faille—nothing shiny). If it's less formality you're after, use cotton curtains. They're simpler, but to my mind not a whit less beautiful.

For upholstered furniture, I use cotton or linen almost exclusively. In a formal room with silk curtains and several damask- or tapestry-covered chairs, I would be inclined to slipcover the upholstered furniture in a print of period design. When you choose upholstery fabric, you should consider two things: durability and flexibility. The ideal—and most expensive—way of doing it is to have the furniture upholstered in muslin and have two sets of slipcovers made, one for fall and winter, one for spring and summer. The next best would be to have upholstery of very tough, hard-wearing, easy-to-clean fabric like denim, linen, or cotton velvet, with a set of lighter-weight slipcovers for change. My own sofa is covered with a white fabric nearly an eighth of an inch thick, handwoven in Nantucket. It's woven from a tough, flaxlike fiber called ramie. All you have to do is draw your fingers across it to feel its stubborn determination to wear. That fabric will outlast me, I'm sure. But even with the very sturdiest fabrics, it is wise to have loose cushions upholstered in muslin, then slipcovered in the upholstery fabric so they at least can be zipped off to the cleaners. And have some wide, deep antimacassars made to tuck over arms and pin invisibly along the outside seams. Lighter-weight cottons like chintz don't hold up well as upholstery, and should really be reserved for slipcovers.

For seats of small chairs and benches, and especially for walls, I have a lot of respect for vinyl. When you need practicality and durability, vinyl is the answer. I love real leather, too, and use it often. Leather improves in looks and comfort as it ages.

If you have active children, dogs, or friends who like to sit with one foot under them (an awful habit, but all too common today), you can't expect the upholstery to look good very long if it's in a pale color. Or, for that matter, too dark, either. Neutrals are best—beige and warm browns and grays. If you think that's too drab, you can brighten it up with pillows. As far as I'm concerned, however, I don't think neutrals are at all drab. Just the opposite. A neutral room in a variety of textures can be the most beautiful of all.

Draping the walls with fabric gives instant warmth against the chill of a dreary city. Mr. and Mrs. William Paley's sitting room is entirely enveloped in paisley cotton, shirred for sound control and coziness, colored a rich glowing brown to counteract the harsh city light. It also happens to make a charming background for their eighteenth-century French chairs and wonderful collection of objects.

One room I worked on was exclusively in neutral shades of beiges and browns, with some black and white. Walls were paneled with pale wood. Neutral jute sofas and club chairs sat on a highly polished brown-vinyl floor, with furry rugs in animal shapes in major seating areas. Rough wood French country dining chairs had smooth leatherlike vinyl seats. Crisp dark-patterned cotton covered some little chairs and stools. Modern metal chairs had seats of smooth suede. There were lots of pillows, some velvet, some tawny brocade, others of quilted glove leather. Vases and ashtrays were of pottery or old silver, and lampshades were made of real parchment, so even the light was textured. You would hardly call that room drab.

Even a much shorter span of the neutral spectrum can be outrageously beautiful if you play your textures right. There is a room in London whose colors run entirely between bone and amber. Walls are strié bone. Chairs are covered with tawny cotton velvet, a banquette in fat-weave amber linen. There's not even a pattern in sight, yet the room is absolutely delightful—and full of variety.

The texture of materials enhances patterns, deepens and enriches color, adds a whole new dimension to decorating. It never detracts, and always adds. But in special cases, like absolutely monotone rooms, texture can make the difference between vitality and utter death. In the Paris bedroom of Jean Michel Frank, that great French decorator of the thirties, the walls were painted a thick lustrous white with a glow as rich as if cream had been spilled on them. There were creamy parchment chairs, and beams, floors, and window trim of the snowiest bleached wood. Most unusual of all, the big bed was entirely upholstered and spread with plain, unpatterned white needle-point. The room was entirely patternless, entirely colorless, and entirely breathtaking—full of the magic of texture on texture.

How to be
an expert with pattern

In Paris recently, I saw a freshly decorated room with a great collection of antique French chairs. To update them, their intricately patterned tapestry covers had been replaced with plain-colored satin ones. A friend of

One bold pattern, lavished everywhere, makes Mr. and Mrs. Frederick Guest's octagonal bedroom look as if the woods outside had suddenly swept in, spiced with clear, fresh, straight-out-of-the-tube colors, and laced with white. My one fear was that my clients would be driven mad by the ceiling—a circular one with a clear glass dome smack in the center. I couldn't have been more wrong; the stars are their ceiling, they say, and it's the most romantic thing in the world during a snowfall.

mine, a woman with marvelous taste, saw the finished room, too. "It is obviously very expensive, but an utter bore," she said. "It is absolutely patternless. There is nothing for your eye to feed on."

In my own experience, I have learned that to omit pattern or texture from a room is to leave it looking flavorless. "Lots of pattern makes a room too busy," protest novices, not sure of themselves. They forget pattern-on-pattern is nature's way.

In decorating, these are two ways I use pattern: a little or a lot. When you use a lot, you create the currently popular pattern-on-pattern room, where practically no surface is left untouched by pattern of one sort or another. Such clutters of pattern look best in small rooms, because small rooms and lots of pattern have the same kind of intimate quality about them.

Paisley on paisley splashed on at Kenneth's salon. My inspiration was that marvelous pleasure palace, the Brighton Pavilion. The material is cotton—yards and yards of it, used really on a mammoth scale. We swagged it, draped it, tented it, all of it richly colored—scarlet, blue, butter yellow—and filled and surrounded with layer upon layer of pattern. I thought it would be great fun for a woman to have her hair dried under a paisley tent, above, her fingertips manicured on a Porthault pillow, her hair curled by the light of a palm-tree lamp, opposite page, as she sits in a lacquered bamboo chair. Apparently it is indeed fun; I'm told a woman will keep dentists and dinner dates waiting before she'll miss an appointment at Kenneth's.

One day I was sitting with a friend in a room I had decorated with him. We were just relaxing and talking, when suddenly he exclaimed, "Do you realize these patterns in reds and golds just happened to create the kind of atmosphere we were looking for: coziness, feet-up relaxation, a place where you feel coddled." Pattern-on-pattern has a way of doing that.

In a larger room, so much pattern would be either dreary or so overpowering it would knock you down. In such rooms, I like clean, open spaces, expanses of fresh, clear colors, and a little pattern for spice. In a blue and white room I did in France, the pattern is limited to rugs, ottomans, sofa cushions, and a collection of Chinese porcelains. If you were to eliminate any of the pattern, the room would look rather antiseptic. But any more pattern would be just too fussy.

Whichever way you use pattern, the one great pitfall to avoid is timidity. Many women, in a burst of decorating energy, will put up patterned walls, patterned curtains, patterned furniture, then screech to a halt and install plain carpeting.

You must have the courage to go the limit with pattern. Have a figured carpet or a stenciled floor, or at least the regular, monotone pattern of waxed quarry tiles. And for good measure, heap that flowery sofa with cushions—dozens of them—in lots of tiny prints.

A friend once said to me about a room I had decorated, "Do you realize there are eight different patterns in this room?" Well I didn't realize it. I had to start counting. It certainly was not a pattern-on-pattern room. The walls were white, the floor a dark-brown tile. There were wooden shutters instead of curtains—no pattern there. And the biggest pieces of upholstered furniture were covered with cream-colored linen. But grouped around the fireplace was a cluster of little chairs, benches, and stools, and sure enough, each was covered with a different cotton print.

When I was working on the room, the patterns seemed so natural that I didn't even realize I was using so many. Looking back, I can see that if the little chairs had been covered instead with plain fabric, the room would have looked somehow "unseasoned." There would have been a noticeable gap that only pattern could fill. To have covered them all exactly alike would have been a bore. Needless to say, these patterns were not overpowering or everyone would have noticed them instantly. They were all in the same tawny shades of brown, cream, and black. They were all tiny—either regular little flowers or sharp geometrics. Yet they were by no means pallid or nebulous. They were crisp and bold. It was just that as a whole they blended so well into the room that they did their job inconspicuously.

The only way you can really learn how to use pattern is by training your eye. Get yourself accustomed to looking at good pattern-on-pattern, and let your eye, rather than your mind, absorb the way patterns relate to one another. Take a look around. It will suddenly strike you that the whole world is pattern-on-pattern. Spend some time at a gallery or even with a few books on Oriental and Middle Eastern art or decorating or even fashion. The Japanese, Arabians, Indians, and their neighbors are experts with pattern, putting the most exiting prints together with artless perfection.

Then study the paintings of Vuillard, with their innumerable patterns in simple, often somber, colors. Or the work of Matisse, the master of brilliantly colored pattern. Let your eyes evaluate, and learn to distinguish good pattern combinations from bad. Little by little you begin to get the idea. An Indian necklace will suddenly seem tacky on a solid colored dress, and wildly beautiful on a patterned one—which is, after all, the way it was intended to be worn. You will discover that a painting takes on new vitality when you hang it on a wallpapered wall.

When you walk into a room and one of the patterns strikes your eyes before the others, you will realize instinctively that it doesn't belong there. But you will set a vase of flowers on a table covered with a flowered cloth against a flowered wall, and the three elements, almost insignificant by themselves, will become a unified whole of incredible beauty. Great blends of pattern, like great dishes, must be carefully tasted. And constant tasting is what teaches a cook how to taste.

How to choose furniture to live with

The quality that makes furniture design durable, whether you're talking about a Louis XV armoire or a modern upholstered chair, is its absolute suitability. It must do its intended job effectively, comfortably, and beautifully. Sometimes the piece of furniture that would be exactly suitable just doesn't exist. It is to fill these voids that most good furniture is designed.

The open tubular-brass bookshelves I designed for Cole Porter's library—a room that has since become famous—were born out of just such a need. To begin with, in that room, the vast collection of books was so outstanding that it outshone everything else. There were books on art and architecture, remarkable for the range and taste they reflected, and rare volumes on Chinese porcelains, sculpture, and painting. Books by Maugham, D. H. Lawrence, and other contemporaries of the Porters were each charmingly inscribed. There were beautiful travel books, and a dictionary in every conceivable language, which Cole used when he was composing the lyrics to his songs. There in the library Cole would sit, literally surrounded by books, quietly notating his melodies before taking them to the piano in the next room (he preferred this commuting arrangement to composing at the keyboard).

My problem, then, was what to do with all those books. I thought at first of installing old wood paneling, with sections devoted to the books. But that just seemed too simple for a vital and creative man like Cole. Then my eyes fell on a simple brass Directoire étagère that I had brought in for his sheet music. How wonderful that would be as a bookcase, I thought aloud. Cole's response stunned me: "Why don't you build a whole room out of it?" We did, and it turned out to be a perfect setting for Cole as well as a personal thrill for me.

At that time there was simply no such thing as a contemporary brass bookcase. And the shelves had several advantages that have kept them popular right up until today. They cost far less than built-in bookcases in antique panels. And they are not permanent installations, which makes it a simple matter to move them around the room or even out the door. I have since had the very same design made up in iron and in steel with gilded bronze fittings. The shelves in Cole's bookcases were of ebony; today they can be anything: lacquer, glass, Formica, even bronze Plexiglas. My shelves have been copied by everyone under the sun. People often ask me, in fact, if it bothers me that other designers copy my designs. My answer is a quote from Ruby Ross Wood: "It's when they stop copying you that it's time to worry."

Later I developed another bookcase, a frame of thick square lengths of wood wrapped with strips of willow and inset shelves of Formica-topped wood. The inspiration came from a wonderful raffia-wrapped chair by the great decorator and furniture designer Jean Michel Frank. I liked the bookcases so much that I adapted the idea for tables and benches that resemble the famous Parsons table with legs and apron of wrapped willow and tops of any suitable material. I have two in my own apartment: one a low, narrow bench topped with padded leather, the other a big writing table with a flush top of bronze glass lined with black-painted wood. Wrapped willow, I have found, also makes beautiful tubs for plants.

When it comes to upholstered furniture, I have always preferred big modern fully upholstered sofas, loveseats, and chairs to the wood-framed and leggy period ones, simply because they give the room muscle and character, and are infinitely more comfortable. Of course there are degrees of comfort even in upholstered furniture. For instance, the most comfortable loveseats never measure less than four and one-half feet between the arms. Otherwise you find yourself sitting as if you were in a last-class airplane seat, knees straight ahead of you. The most comfortable filling for loose sofa cushions is not exclusively down, as has long been held, but a core of foam rubber sandwiched between two outer layers of down. The foam gives the cushion bounce and body, so as you sit you don't get that uneasy characteristic-of-down sensation that you might go all the way to the floor. And having the foam in the middle makes the cushion reversible.

When I moved into my studio apartment, I had to think of some kind of bed that would serve equally comfortably and beautifully as a sofa. I hadn't heard of anything on the market that would exactly fill the bill. First, I got myself a very good standard twin-size mattress, and put it on a frame. Then I added the "upholstered head" and footboards that became high arms with fat, loose cushions, slipcovered with upholstery fabric, leaning against them. To reduce the depth of the bed by day and make it look and "sit" more like a sofa, three more down-filled cushions were placed against the wall. I made absolutely certain the design would enable me to keep the bed perpetually made up with sheets and blankets. The bedspread is nothing more elaborate than a piece of upholstery fabric stitched up like a slipcover with a flap that tucks under the mattress.

In all the time I have been planning rooms with lots of modern upholstered furniture, only one annoyance has cropped up: Inevitably, especially with white or pale-color upholstery, a line of dark scuff marks appears about two inches from the floor. This is unavoidable even when yours are the most considerate of guests (I reserve comment on those thoughtless people who insist on tucking one shod foot under them as they sit down on my white sofa.) One way to prevent the unsightly marks is to sew a broad strip of dark braid all around the furniture two inches from the bottom.

Although it's true that a period settee can never replace an upholstered sofa or loveseat as the foundation of a room, please don't outlaw them. A beautiful thing of the past, or even a good reproduction, seems to complement a modern room with modern furniture, giving it a sense of warmth and establishment as well as very charming and often necessary visual variety.

The same kind of visual variety can also be achieved in another way—by not having any two tables in a room, unless they're a pair, exactly the same height. In my apartment, I have a very old Portuguese table thirty inches high, another table twenty-eight inches high that I use as a bar, a very big writing table, and for contrast, two coffee tables. The coffee tables are usually low, and some people find them inconvenient, but that's the way they came, and I think they fit the room perfectly. In general, however, fifteen inches is the best coffee-table height.

Some years back it occurred to me that it might be a good idea to try to combine into one design the comfort of a fully upholstered chair with the portability of a stool or lightweight wooden side chair. In the 1930's when I was working for Ruby Ross Wood, we developed from the popular long-armed Lawson sofa a big armless chair, so massive that one person could relax on it quite luxuriously and it could easily seat two at a cocktail party. Using this armless Lawson as a jumping-off point, I pared it down, experimented by trial and error with the pitch of the back, and finally produced what is now known as the Lawson slipper chair. It is a small, low, armless chair, but with remarkable versatility. Small women and football linebackers find it equally comfortable. It can be covered in anything from leather for a man's study to pink flowered chintz for a lady's bathroom and still look good. Several of them can be used in one room and not make it look the least bit like a movie house. In my own tiny living room, I have no fewer than four, all slipcovered to the floor with perfectly flat, fitted, pleatless skirts. I think they are my favorite chairs of all. They are light as a feather, and people find it easy to drag them about. Those little chairs have a way of making everyone feel at home.

The pleasure
of beautiful
carpets and rugs

Last fall in my one-room apartment, I made the most conspicuous change short of total redecoration. I got rid of my wall-to-wall carpeting and bought a rug. The whole production brought to mind that the choice between wall-to-wall and rugs has very little to do with right and wrong, and everything to do with fashion, taste, even a bit of restlessness for change.

For my apartment, either wall-to-wall carpeting or a rug is perfectly acceptable. I have had it both ways, and loved both. Carpeting gave the room a smoothed-out, united look, a warm feeling, and the soundlessness of a monk's cell. Now, I have sacrificed the absolute stillness for the sparkle of a polished wood floor, a feeling of space, a clean, sharp look, and a real beauty of a handloomed Nantucket rug.

Throughout history, rugs have been the glory of decorating, and today we have a lavish choice: the wonderful pale, flat-piled beige and brown Samarkands, the most beautiful of the Orientals, which go with almost any furniture style. The almost-too-grand Aubussons of eighteenth-century France that must be used in very small sips, such as by a fire or beside a bed—unless, of course, you own palace furniture. The eighteenth- and nineteenth-century Bessarabians, coarser than the others, with flaming colors and a great deal of black, very much suited to the way we decorate today. Moroccans—wonderful beige, black, and white geometrics that can bring together a roomful of oddments (you can often turn up a beauty even today). Iranian rugs, very native looking, and, like American Indian rugs, wonderful with modern furniture.

You can't beat carpeting for quiet and luxury in bedrooms and dressing rooms, even in the country. And it's just about the only way to cover a floor that's beyond hope and would be too costly to replace. But even when you must have carpeting, you needn't forfeit rugs. You can easily cover a freaked-out floor with a rug, stretching it to touch the walls with a sewn-on, solid-colored border. Or you can simply pretend that a nice, flat neutral or small-patterned carpet is the floor and put wonderful rugs on top of it. Designer David Hicks revolutionized the floors of the world with his carpets of small geometric patterns that take the place of solid color.

On an uncarpeted floor, there are several places where a rug is essential. A rug helps to define a seating area and make it look more inviting. Beside a bed, a rug cozies toes even in summer. A rug is a delight for lounging on by the fire and a must in the dining room, under the table. There, a rug really helps keep down the noise level and is much pleasanter for the feet than a hard floor. By no means should a dining-room rug be thick or shaggy—it ought to be flat, smooth, and easy to clean. Another requirement: A dining-room rug should be large enough so that all four legs of every chair stand squarely on top of it, even when you push away from the table. Few small annoyances are more irritating than having to hoist your chair over the edge of a rug every time you change position.

Every rug should have a border of some sort—either worked right into the design or sewn on. Otherwise it looks as if it were cut from a roll, giving the whole room a kind of unfinished look. Staircase runners, too, should be bordered on each side, and hallway runners all the way around. And every rug needs a rubber mat under it. A mat can be cut as easily as piecrust dough; it keeps the rug from slipping, makes it softer, and prolongs its life.

Today we have an unlimited choice of materials to suit where the rug is to be used. For instance, lacy Portuguese straw lets a brilliant lacquered floor shine through. Raffia and sisal are woven flat into squares that are sewn together into rugs of any size you need—even wall to wall. For bedrooms in summer, cotton and linen fibers, woven in herringbone patterns, are as soft as they are cool. And for a spot in a doorway or by a fire, there is our old standby, needlepoint.

Sometimes the perfect rug was never meant to be used on the floor, or, conversely, some great rugs never touch a floor. On one Long Island porch, paved with gray flagstones and furnished with white wicker and red geraniums, the rug is actually a tent hanging from Tunisia. And in a New York library I once visited, soft tapestry rugs, beautifully woven in a fine geometric, glorified not the floor, but every piece of upholstered furniture in sight.

Shopping for rugs is not an easy task. There are so many dazzlers around that being forced to choose only one or two of them is a minor ordeal. Nevertheless, my advice is to see as many as you can, especially the great ones. Looking at rugs can be as lavish a feast for your eyes as looking at paintings, and no one who loves beauty should miss either.

First step to a beautiful room— the floor plan

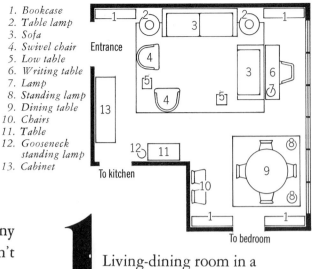

1. Bookcase
2. Table lamp
3. Sofa
4. Swivel chair
5. Low table
6. Writing table
7. Lamp
8. Standing lamp
9. Dining table
10. Chairs
11. Table
12. Gooseneck standing lamp
13. Cabinet

The bone structure of any room is its preliminary floor plan. If the floor plan isn't right, you may end up with a superficially pretty room, but one where comfort is only skin deep. If you skip the floor plan altogether, the result can be total confusion. You'll buy too much of the wrong furniture, and you'll have to arrange it by grueling trial and error.

The first thing I do when I am asked to work on a room my clients have not yet moved into is to measure the walls and ceiling height, check the exposures, and see about the adequacy of electrical sockets. Then I go back to the family's present home and survey the furniture they're planning to take along. Having in mind a few pieces of furniture, as well as the characteristics of the room, often suggests the beginnings of a comfortable arrangement. Of course, when I am taken to an empty room and told that everything will have to be bought new, I have only the room itself to plan from. But I never draw a plan before I am thoroughly sure of the way the room is to be lived in.

To demonstrate the way a floor plan works, I have chosen three plans representing quite ordinary rooms, and arranged them with furniture for multipurpose living, which is the way most people like to live nowadays. Two of the plans are for typical city apartments. The third might be found in a country house. In drawing up a furniture-arrangement plan, we are not in the least concerned with color, fabrics, kind of curtains, or doorknobs, or any other incidentals. This is strictly business.

1 Living-dining room in a city apartment

This is the living-dining room of a typical New York one-bedroom apartment: low ceiling, no fireplace, and only a single exposure. My imaginary clients have two requirements: places for their books and someplace to write.

For the books, I plan four big bookcases, two in the dining area to create the atmosphere of a dining-library, one within easy access of the writing table, and the other near the front door. The bookcases, which reach to the ceiling, stand on top of low cupboards for music equipment. The writing table backs up to a short sofa. The window will provide general, glareless daylight, but a lamp on the table will give good working light. I feel very strongly that a writing chair be very comfortable—preferably with arms.

The conversation area as well as the writing table has a clear view of the television, which shares the cabinet beside the front door with table, linens, silver, and liquor. The cabinet could be tall like an armoire or low enough for a painting to hang above it. The upholstered armchairs nearby are set on swivels so they may face the television or the sofas. All the upholstered furniture in the conversation area is arranged on the rug, which defines the area and makes it visually more snug.

Tucked away in a corner of the room is the dining table, which can seat six people comfortably for meals, or four for a game of cards. It is entirely lighted by a pair of standing lamps, either direct or indirect. The rug under the table helps muffle noise as well as isolate the area from the rest of the room.

Beside the kitchen door, within easy reach of living and dining areas, stands a table, where the grog tray may be at the ready.

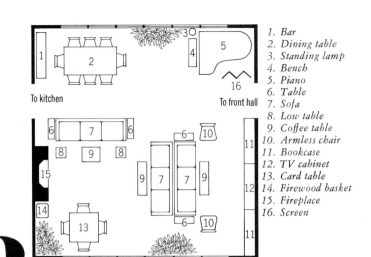

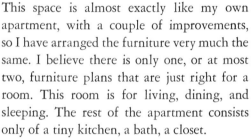

1. Dining chair
2. Bookcase
3. Standing lamp
4. Ottoman
5. Sofa
6. Coffee table
7. Armless chair
8. Table and lamp
9. Sofa bed
10. TV in low cabinet
11. Lamp
12. Writing table
13. Armchair
14. Card-dining table
15. Cabinet and bar

1. Bar
2. Dining table
3. Standing lamp
4. Bench
5. Piano
6. Table
7. Sofa
8. Low table
9. Coffee table
10. Armless chair
11. Bookcase
12. TV cabinet
13. Card table
14. Firewood basket
15. Fireplace
16. Screen

2 One-room apartment in the city

This space is almost exactly like my own apartment, with a couple of improvements, so I have arranged the furniture very much the same. I believe there is only one, or at most two, furniture plans that are just right for a room. This room is for living, dining, and sleeping. The rest of the apartment consists only of a tiny kitchen, a bath, a closet.

First, to take advantage of the crosslight from all the windows, I mirrored the wall around the corner from the kitchen door, then tucked the sofa bed and two narrow tables into the niche. Across from the sofa bed and backing up to the long writing table is the television, set in a low cabinet with door so I can let TV into my life at my convenience. To make the sleeping area more sociable for waking hours, I put in four little upholstered armless chairs. Behind the writing table, a huge bookcase with books from floor to ceiling.

To the left of the writing table is my "invisible" dining area, where the only stationary furniture is the low cabinet, topped with a grog tray, with door and drawers for silver, linens, and liquor. Flanking it are two dining chairs and, above them, a pair of wall-hung lamps. Two more dining chairs stand beside the bookcase and beside the kitchen door. For dining or cards, the folding table whips out of the closet.

I put a long sofa and a pair of leafy potted trees in front of the windows at the end of the room because that looked like such a sunny, inviting place to sit. And it turned out to be a good idea. Whenever someone comes to visit, they invariably head straight for that sofa.

3 Living-dining room in a contemporary country house

This is my favorite kind of room: Everything about it is ideal! It's a perfect square. The doors are in the right places. There are big beautiful windows on opposite sides, and a fireplace to boot. And the ceiling is twelve feet high. All the night light is to come from recessed ceiling spots, which will be located after the furniture plan is approved, so everything will be perfectly lighted.

In arranging the furniture, I wanted to do three things: preserve the feeling of spaciousness and light, make the room as versatile as possible so everyone would want to spend a lot of time there, and, of course, make it all dreamily comfortable.

Instead of having lots of cluttery little chairs around, the plan includes three long rambling sofas and, facing the entertainment and book wall, two big armless upholstered chairs that can easily seat two each. Yet an assortment of low coffee and end tables put everyone within easy distance of his drink. The entertainment wall itself consists of three low cabinets, the television and music equipment in the center, storage for records, linen, and silver to the right and left. Above the side cabinets, books to the ceiling. Above the TV, space for a wonderful modern painting.

The dining table in the opposite corner will seat eight people comfortably, and the permanent game table across from it will seat four more. The nice thing about that little table is that it can be left near the window on balmy summer days when the garden is blooming, or, on wintry days, drawn up near the fire. The game chairs are to be very luxurious upholstered armchairs that can be pulled over to the conversation area near the sofas.

Solving problems with floor plans

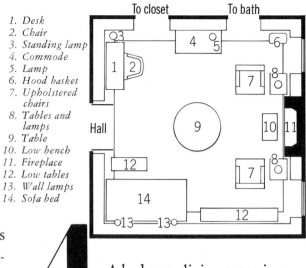

1. Desk
2. Chair
3. Standing lamp
4. Commode
5. Lamp
6. Hood basket
7. Upholstered chairs
8. Tables and lamps
9. Table
10. Low bench
11. Fireplace
12. Low tables
13. Wall lamps
14. Sofa bed

It would be a decorator's dream if every room were flawless, with perfectly proportioned ceilings and walls, well-placed doors and windows, fine square corners, and just the proper details to suit its owners' intended purpose. Alas, a room like this is very hard to come by.

In New York apartments and all over the country, the general rule is low ceilings, tiny spaces, windows cramped in corners or all on one wall, and odd protuberances jutting from walls and ceiling in the most untidy way. Or if the room itself is acceptable, the client may complicate matters by specifying needs that are beyond the naked room's basic capabilities. On the other hand, a room's idiosyncracies might just be the beginnings of greatness: a breathtaking view through glorious windows, or enough floor space for a set of tennis, or a soared, arched ceiling. But even when you have a room with a marvelous potential you owe it careful thought and planning to avoid disaster: You don't want a tennis-court-sized room to come off looking like a tennis court.

To show how I might handle a few such problems, I have prepared three furniture plans for rooms with tricky peculiarities of one sort or another. In rooms like these, floor plans are doubly essential; their bird's-eye view of the situation gives a much better overall view than simply standing in the room. The plans, I hope, solve the problems, emphasize the good features, and meet the clients' needs: comfort and style.

4 A bedroom-living room in a town house library

This is really a fairly nice room: a generous square with a big fireplace and entirely lined with built-in bookshelves, even above the doors and windows. The tricky parts are that it has only one exposure and literally not an inch of vacant wall space, and that it must be furnished for comfortable living and sleeping.

To make room for furniture along the walls, I suppose I could have removed a few sections of bookshelves. But that would have destroyed the graceful symmetry of the room. And besides, I think books—and the more the better—are the greatest asset to any room. So I decided to leave the shelves and merely treat them as if they were bare walls wherever necessary, then filling in with books.

In a square room, I like to have a piece of furniture smack in the center, to unify the room and emphasize its good natural balance. In this case it's a table four feet across and round, because round tables seem to go with you as you walk. It's the kind of table you might put books or magazines, the mail, or a pot of flowers on. It is not meant for dining. Another room-unifier is the square rug, showing a border of good floor all around.

The room has two sitting areas. The main one is the fireplace: a pair of large-scale reading chairs, each with its own generous table and reading lamp, and a low bench that could be sat upon, drawn up as a footstool, or used as a table for the Sunday newspaper. The other is the sofa bed, with its combination coffee-bedside table, and the armchair from the desk across the room, which could really be pulled up anywhere it is needed.

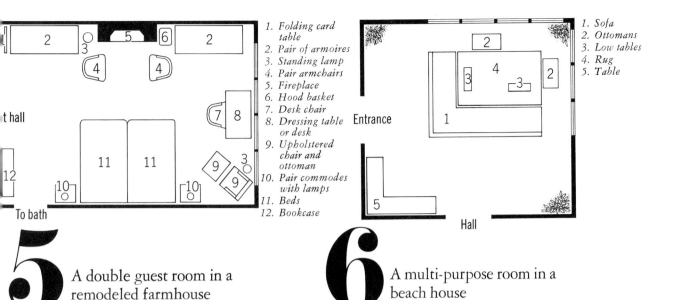

5 A double guest room in a remodeled farmhouse

Guests are likely to stay at least a week, so the room must be very comfortable indeed, with as many conveniences as possible. The fireplace adds enormously to the luxury of the room, as do the sliding glass doors, which open onto a garden. There is only one hitch—and it's a big one. There is no dressing room, indeed not even a hint of a closet of any kind.

The first thing I included, therefore, was a pair of armoires, very tall and six feet wide, with shelves and hanging space inside to fill the walls flanking the fireplace.

On the opposite wall are the big, oversized beds, each four feet wide by six-and-a-half feet long. These could be separated or used together as one palatial bed. Each has its own generous bedside commode and lamp.

The single-drawered writing table at the window is designed to double as a dressing table with the simple addition of a standing mirror on top. Beside the table, a deeply comfortable upholstered reading chair plus ottoman gets its light from the window, or, at night, the low metal-shaded standing lamp beside it. Across the room, by the door, books fill a tall glass-and-steel bookcase.

Standing before the fireplace are two open armchairs, quite comfortable, and just the right height for breakfasting by a crackling fire on wintry mornings. For such breakfasts, a folding card table is kept handy in the corner beside the left-hand armoire. To make a smooth, continuous background for the masses of furniture and to add even more to the luxury of the room, I think this room should have wall-to-wall flaxen carpeting—flat, soft.

6 A multi-purpose room in a beach house

Its great attribute is obvious—those huge windows practically filling two walls, making a marvelous panorama of the moors and sea. Looking at this room, I can't help thinking of it as white, the color of purity, light, and space.

The decorating problem here is that this space must serve as an entrance hall and a living room as well. So, with the idea of adding living-room comforts while maintaining the room's feeling of great space, I decided to use a minimum of furniture, all of it massive and low. The dominating piece of furniture is an enormous L-shaped sofa with loose seat and back cushions, deep and full, yet only twenty-four inches tall overall. Anyone standing anywhere in the room can look right over it to the wonderful view beyond. The two lacquered coffee tables are very low indeed, and instead of chairs with eye-impeding backs and arms, there is in front of each window a wicker ottoman topped with a cushion. To control glare and light, there are Roman shades that pull down from behind ceiling pockets.

Positioning the sofa so its two axes line up with the ends of the windows, as well as being visually balanced, allows traffic between the front door and the rest of the house to flow unimpeded and without interrupting the living area. A rug completes the rectangle.

To reflect the light and view, the two walls forming the corner opposite the windows are entirely mirrored. Against them stands a lacquer-topped L-shaped wicker table. The remaining walls should be reserved for beautiful things to see—large abstract paintings, sculpture, potted flowers and greens.

How to
turn your house on
with lighting

Not long ago I was in a room as dimly lighted as a movie house. I could just barely see the faces of the people sitting beside me. Most likely our hostess thought the lighting was romantic. It was merely inadequate. As Ruby Ross Wood once said to me, "There is one fundamental fact about lighting: Where there is no light, there is no beauty." On the other hand, some people think brightly colored rooms must be brilliantly lighted. But flooding a room with light washes out the color and flattens all the nuances of shape and texture. Too much light is as oppressive as a bare bulb hanging down from the ceiling. The perfectly lighted room is subtly lighted.

Light is, first and last, for seeing. It's what you are trying to see that dictates the kind of lamp you buy and where you put it. For reading, for instance, the worst possible light is unfortunately the most common: a big, tall lamp with a translucent shade so the light shines right smack in your eyes. A reading lamp should be below eye level, with an opaque shade that confines the light to your book. And not too strong a light, please—that bright white page can create almost as uncomfortable a glare as the light itself.

In the dining room, the primary source of light should not be, as so many people assume, the chandelier. A chandelier is a beautiful thing, but people ruin it by putting in the brightest bulbs they can find. Then it becomes garish and distracting and very uncomfortable. Even the light reflected by the silver on the table can be a pinpoint in your eye. Ideally, the chandelier lights should be just bright enough to make the prisms sparkle. Most of the light to see by should come from soft spots in the ceiling with perhaps a few candles—again, below eye level—to give all the faces a glow.

One of the worst evenings I ever spent was in a dining room exclusively lighted by spotlights focused on four or five paintings on the walls. It was terrifying to eat at that dim table with those ghastly luminous pictures staring down. What the hostess wanted was to be sure everyone noticed her art collection. But the light was too strong—the paintings looked like cheap, lighted glass. Lighting pictures is tricky anyway. One of the best ways is to wash a whole wall with a very soft light. Then you can rearrange the pictures without worrying about readjusting the lights. But the lighting must be extremely subtle. You should not even be aware that there is a light shining on the picture—until you turn it off.

In a hallway or on a staircase, the most logical place for light is where your feet are—on the floor. In one of the most attractive halls I know—walls of rough wood, floor of the same wood but whitened and polished—the light comes from a narrow cove just above the baseboard molding. You are led forward by the light, and you almost feel as if the floor is warm, actually carpeted with light. Most staircases are so dark they are just a hazard. If they're lighted at all, it's with a bulb at the top of the stairwell, forcing you to flounder up and down the stairs in an atmosphere as spooky as a haunted house. Why not light the steps along the sides, like that baseboard-lighted hallway? Or light each step by a light on the underside of the tread above.

Lighting the living room is the most fun because the function of lamps is really to decorate the room with light. That doesn't mean that you run out and buy the most ornate lamps you can find. Nor does it mean having your favorite teapot made into a lamp. The great value of a lamp is as a giver of light, not as an artistic medium. Now there is a wealth of beautiful, almost architecturally designed lamps to be found. I applaud them—glowing shapes in Plexiglas, chrome columns that throw light at the ceiling, wonderful sculptures with lights in them. They are beautiful in themselves, yet they begin and end as a means of giving light.

To me, the epitome of decorating with light is in a chateau in France where all the furniture is arranged as if it were objects on a table. All through the large living room are little groupings of chairs and tables and flowers lighted by slim silver electrified candlesticks with the smallest possible paper shades. The light is softly spotted, silhouetting a chair against a table, casting lovely shadows. At the end of the room is a fireplace where a fire is always burning—the most wonderful light of all.

Nothing makes a room sparkle like mirror

Mirror is mysterious. In large shimmering sheets, it can change the shape and size of a room. In small flashes, it can catch the sparkle of light the way a jewel catches the sun. Mirror is by nature glamorous and gay. It makes things bigger—or at least I have never know it to make things smaller. Yet you can never really be sure, until it's finally in place, exactly what magic the mirror will make.

As an architectural element, mirror is a most effective material for remodeling a a room without actually knocking down the walls—and it's certainly less expensive. In my own apartment, a veritable jigsaw of angles and corners, all the walls are painted very dark shiny brown, except three panels of mirror from floor to ceiling. I installed one mirror to broaden the room, make it less cramped and more interesting. Another, adjacent to a row of windows, gives the illusion of another window. The third reflects the windows' light. But all that mirror does something extra as well (here's where the magic comes in): At night, when the windows are dark, you can't really tell the difference between the real room and its counterfeit image.

A mirror can double a beautiful view. I once heard of a man who loved a certain river so much he moved into an apartment beside it. Then he mirrored his walls almost scientifically, so that no matter where in his apartment he stood, he could see at least a reflection of his river. I once had an apartment with three tiny windows in a little hall that faced the East River. I mirrored part of the wall across from the windows, and although I can't say I found it necessary to have the East River with me wherever I went, I will admit it was nice to have two views of it for the price of one.

A wonderful trick is to put mirror right at the window. In one city living room, with a less than spectacular view of a side alley, the owners covered all the window reveals with mirror. Then they installed two tiers of folding shutters, wood on the outside, mirror on the inside. With the bottom half closed, the shutters keep out the view, yet reflect sparkle and light from the upper half, making the whole window bright as sunshine. A folding mirrored screen, too, especially if you put it near a window, gives exciting broken reflections and sends the window's light all over the room.

Hallways were meant for mirrors. Cole Porter had the entrance of his Waldorf apartment mirrored everywhere—ceiling and all—except for the black and beige marble floor. It was a dazzling little jewel of a room. On one mirrored wall was a wonderful mirrored barometer. On another, a gilt-framed mirror. The only furniture was a console table, a little chair, and some luxuriant green plants that the mirror transformed into an instant jungle. Inside halls, like the ones that lead to bedrooms or dressing rooms, are exciting if you wall them with mirror. Or you might mirror only the doors in a long hall, to give staccato reflections as you pass. In a dressing room, mirrored doors are marvelous. If you have a pair of closets in a bedroom, you can mirror the inside of each door and be able to see both sides of every situation.

Mirror, like any other good thing, can be overdone. I would never lavish it on a room in which you're trying to establish a certain kind of quiet—a restful room, where you want to think deeply, converse undisturbed, work without distractions.

I would think twice, too, before putting a lot of mirror in a house outside the city. In the city, you dress up a room to make up for a certain lack of natural openness, beautiful views, and fresh air. But I'd never have mirrored entrance halls or shutters in a country house. I'd have treillage and beautiful blowing curtains.

Framed mirrors, of course, are beautiful anywhere. On the Left Bank in Paris, there is a white room twenty feet tall, with three immense windows curtained in red damask facing the Seine. Between them and on each of the other walls hang five towering gilt Louis Quinze mirrors. They are fantastically beautiful to look at, and they also serve, as mirrored walls would, to make the garden, trees, and river outside a living part of the room. Sometimes big mirrors can work wonders even in a small room. A friend of mine has a very tiny but disproportionately tall apartment in New York. It's all painted white and furnished with small-scale furniture in brown suedes and black leather and a beautiful black and white patterned Moroccan rug. Rather than try to minimize the height of the room, my friend decided to exaggerate it: Instead of hanging pictures, on three walls facing tall windows he hung three colossal overscaled Tunisian mirrors framed in pale wood and mother-of-pearl. The result is beautiful—the room's one eccentricity is its greatest asset.

Over a mantel, I usually prefer a mirror to a painting. A mirror above a roaring fire makes a marvelous light, but a picture and a fire somehow compete. In one room, we compromised by hanging above the sofa a beautiful painting carefully placed so that it was framed by the mirror above the mantel across the room. In classical eighteenth-century French rooms, the over-mantel mirror was built right into the boiserie, and opposite it, usually above a console table, was its twin. Over a sofa, I would use only a built-in mirror—or one that looks as if it were. There is something ominous about sitting under a dangling mirror. What's worse is a mirror above a bed.

Sometimes the prettiest thing to do with a framed mirror is to hang it on a mirrored wall—far preferable to hanging a picture there. When you look at a painting surrounded by mirror, you see the reflection of your entire body, with the exception of your head, which makes some people very uncomfortable and amuses others. Either way, the picture loses. In other ways, however, you can treat a mirrored wall just like a painted or papered one. One of my mirrored walls was awful without something on it, so I hung a giant tortoiseshell smack in the middle—to break up the image, yet keep that illusion of depth.

Although I am not fond of large furniture covered with mirror, I do love to see little mirrored tables or stools with mirrored legs. One of the most brilliant uses of mirror I have ever seen on furniture was a hall table designed by Charles Sevigny for the hall of La Fiorentina. The top was a huge rectangular slab six inches deep, finished in dark, rich brown lacquer. It was supported by a pair of completely mirrored blocks, each two feet tall, a foot thick and a yard wide. In the facets of mirror, the Italian marble floor, all intricately patterned beiges and apricots, became fascinating distorted reflections. And the heavy lacquered top seemed suspended in air.

Sometimes the greatest total effect you can get from mirror is to add up a lot of tiny slivers—octagonal flowerpots made of bands of mirror; embroidered pillows with little mirrors sewn in; fragments of mirror, like shining baguettes, on door panels, cornice moldings, and picture frames. As you walk past them the tiny quick twinkles of light catch the corner of your eye, giving the room a feeling of merriment and wit, and beautiful brilliance.

Details
that make the difference

Not everything that makes a room appealing costs a great deal of money. Some things cost a lot of money, some very little, some none at all. These are the details that make the difference between a perfectly nice room and one that is full of life and charm.

For instance: I've always believed that architecture is more important than decoration. Scale and proportion give everlasting satisfaction that cannot be achieved by only icing the cake. But if for some reason you are stuck with ill proportion, it can indeed be disguised by color and furniture arrangement. I've always contended it is possible to make any room charming by applying taste and experience. Not even a large budget is necessary. Take a look at the doors—and particularly the "door furniture" or hardware. If it is either banal or downright ugly, why not remove it? Put in its place the most suitable and decorative hardware—old or new —that you can find. Good hardware will give the room a sense of quality. If you move you can take it with you, but please put the originals safely

Thoroughly scarlet, the library, near right top, *in Mrs. John Wintersteen's Pennsylvania house is one of the coziest rooms I know. There's India chintz on the furniture, a plaid rug, red-flannel curtains, and the most cozying detail of all, a crackling fire. The umbrella stand is Chinese.*

Mrs. Wintersteen's living room, near right bottom, *is a planned mélange of things she loves. The chair is covered with English needlepoint, the sofa in a lovely French cotton damask. There are two little tables that used to be Chinese garden stools. And above the sofa, a glorious Picasso.*

Decorating has never been more personal than in Mrs. Munn Kellogg's house in Palm Beach, where nearly every room reflects the owner's passion for wildlife. In the loggia, far right top, *we mounted her trophies on whitewashed walls and left the room completely devoid of color except for the animals and flowers.*

Orange restored is Mrs. Kellogg's sitting room, with orange-patterned covers for the upholstered furniture and curtains, solid orange for chairs. Animals here, two mammoth elephant tusks, a shaggy lion rug.

away so you can reinstall them, which you must, instead of leaving your beautiful hardware there, which you must not. The same replacement rule applies to lighting fixtures. Very likely a new chandelier or lantern in the entrance hall will not only improve the room esthetically but also give a more agreeable or better light.

The greatest possible improvement you can make is to rip out an ugly mantel and replace it with a good one. Good in design and good in scale, whether contemporary or antique. Again, though, don't forget to keep the original in a safe place, in the basement or even in storage, ready to reinstall if you leave. This may cost some money, but the change will be worth the cost. It's really not very pleasant to sit and look at an ugly mantel any more than it is to sit and look at an ugly picture. And the mantel is usually the focal point of the room.

More details: What gives a room more vitality, looks more welcoming, than a fire in the fireplace? It gives you intimate warmth in winter, kills the chill of evenings in spring. When you are building a new house, a fireplace in the living room would seem a necessity. But what about the luxury of a fireplace in your bedroom, or the super luxury of having one in your bathroom? I once lived in a converted brownstone on the drawing-room floor. My apartment had a small entrance hall with a square living room to the left and a square bedroom to the right. As I came home from work in winter I could see two fires burning, like two hearts beating, one in each room.

A fireplace without a fire can be very unfriendly, especially if the andirons hold three matched birch logs that obviously have never been touched. Of course you can't keep a fire burning all the time, but the hearth should be laid with ordinary logs, kindling etc. so the fire will be all ready to go at the touch of a match. In summer, when you know the fireplace is not going to be used, I think it looks very pretty to do one of two things: In the opening of the fireplace you can set a big basket of greens. Or you can do what they used to do in Europe—replace the mesh screen with an attractive painted fire screen. I've seen some that were very decorative.

Many modern apartments, alas, have no fireplaces at all, but you can still enjoy the vitality of fire by burning candles in charming candlesticks or candelabra in strategic corners of the room. The fire not only adds life, it sheds a glow on flowers and other objects around it. I've just tried this in my own living room. I've put two candles on a table with a number of small objects I could never do anything with. Gilt, brass, crystal, or whatever, they all take on a wonderful aliveness. I can't tell you what has happened to that room—at night it just has a sort of magic. You can use a few candles anywhere you don't want to add a lamp, or can't add a lamp, such as a table in the middle of a room. But to my view there are really only two colors in candles—natural off-white or, for some rooms, black. In my room with its dark walls, I use tall, thin black candles in short Dutch brass holders. And you don't actually see the candles themselves—only flickering flames.

Flowers, too, can make a room come alive. But lovely as all flowers are, it is easily possible to overflower a room. If there is an arrangement on every table, your room can look as if you had received condolence from kind friends. Fewer flowers with space and light showing through them are more natural than too solid masses that look expensive. I don't think any bouquet should look too expensive. The marvelous thing about a flower is that it is alive—a product of nature. Lately, I think, we have overarranged our arrangements so that you hardly see the individual flowers. They never grow that way on a bush or in a bed, but in some arrangements they are so crammed and jammed they seem to be suffocating. On the other hand I knew a great lady decorator, Marian Hall, who always had on her little Louis XVI marble mantel a pair of porcelain cachepots filled with fresh flowers of the season. There were no other bouquets in the room so the cachepots became the most ravishing living objects. They were perfectly marvelous because they didn't crowd the mantel, and the flowers didn't smell too much. They just sat there looking absolutely lovely. This woman had been using these cachepots thus, to my knowledge since 1935. She moved several times but always they reappeared filled with fresh flowers on the mantel of her living room —the most personal touch in the world.

Recently I have been sending people plants. Sometimes plants will blossom a second time, but usually they are charming after the flowers on them have faded. And I don't feel that pots of necessity must be hidden by baskets. Often the color of natural terra-cotta pots is lovely, especially with a little bit of moss on them. They look exactly as though they had come straight out of the greenhouse into your room. If you have a friend who lives in a traditional room with modern overtones or in a totally modern room, a single potted orchid is a sure bet. Lately, I've been using the little pale-green orchids, some dark-brown ones that look like lacquer, or the yellow butterfly ones. They are the most ravishing decoration—they get to be like a wonderful little piece of porcelain or sculpture.

"The Things I Love"

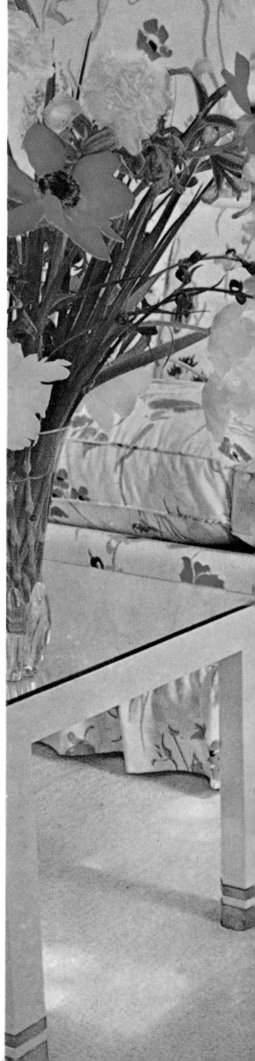

- **Clean, clean color.**

- **Brilliant flower colors.**
  Flowers on white background wallpaper,
  flowers on white background cotton,
  fresh flowers always.

- **Lots of white.**

- **A country house look
  in the city.**

- **Cotton everywhere —**
  never expensive-looking.
  Cotton, like all simple things,
  is at home anywhere.

Off-white
textured materials —
rough linen, handwoven cottons,
unsilky raw silk.

The look of comfort —
comfort, based upon
the use of the room
with beautiful furniture
comfortably arranged.

Curtains as simple as possible.

Curtains brought down to today in cotton, linen, sailcloth, raw silk, and always made to draw.

Off-white rugs and carpets –

onderful oatmeal color
braided linen, and
ncut pile in small designs
ke needlepoint. *Or* pale,
at subtle Orientals.

● The Banquette —

as sofa, for meals or the card table.

● The best possible upholstered furniture,

preferably slip-covered,

for practical reasons and the look of ease. The solidity of furniture upholstered straight to the floor, eliminating the leggy look. The use of small-scale upholstered chairs, easily moved.

The elegance of simplicity and honesty.

Rooms suitable for their use
created with an awareness
of budget and maintenance cost.

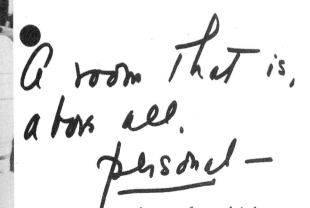

A room that is, above all, personal —

a mixture of people's loves
and memorabilia of living.
A room that looks like
"a joy" in the creating.

A room should be
equally appetizing
when filled with people
or when you're alone there.
It's you and your taste
that make
a room seductive.

5

THE BONES OF A BEAUTIFUL ROOM

THE BONES OF A BEAUTIFUL ROOM

An open-and-shut case for great doors

In the villa La Fiorentina in the South of France, there is a large square hall, lovely enough in its own right, but made absolutely fascinating by its four pairs of huge double doors. One pair is the entrance doors, heavy ones painted in faux bois with marvelous trompe l'oeil panels and moldings. Directly opposite is an identical pair of doors that are always kept wide open. Through them you see the drawing room, and beyond it, through another broad opening shielded by two fabulous Coromandel screens, a charming little stair hall. To your right is a pair of glass doors giving onto a grove of olives. And to your left are the dining-room doors, also faux bois, but always kept closed. Open, they would give the hall three distinct views, dissolving its identity as a room in itself. Besides, I think it's a lovely custom to keep the dining room a secret until dinnertime. Then, with the table set and the flowers arranged, the doors are opened to a beautiful surprise. Once inside, you close them again, to protect the dining room from the noise and activity of the outside world.

Whether or not doors should be open or closed has a lot to do with how you feel about it, how it makes the room look, and inevitably, whether the rest of the family will abide by your decision. So many clients say they'd adore keeping the doors closed, but are resigned to the fact that they'll always be open. Although I love the casualness of this very American open-door policy, I also respect the Europeans' habit of closing doors to make each room an entity. A closed room contains not only the people but also the conversation and the concentration and acts as a fortress against outside disturbance. When you have a houseguest, closed doors give both of you the freedom to come and go without feeling obliged to greet each other every time you

Pattern on the door gives a big lift to Mrs. Clive Runnells' Florida foyer. This one started out as old Spanish oak (and still is, on the outside). The inside we gave several coats of white enamel, made a pattern with masking tape in a simplified version of the one in the old Moroccan rug, and painted between the taped edges. Anyone could do it, and the effect is tremendous.

132

Overleaf: A curtained eighteenth-century bed in the house of Mr. and Mrs. William McCormick Blair, Jr.

pass a doorway. Closed doors help keep certain rooms—like libraries and bedrooms—sanctuaries of peace. And they are always a reminder, especially to children, to knock. Privacy is one of our last remaining luxuries, but fast becoming as polluted as air and water, and as rare as silence. In a big room with double doors, it is often attractive to leave just one of the pair open. The closed door then serves as a kind of screen, so you come upon the room little by little, like the broadening panorama of the Mediterranean as you drive around a mountain. From inside, the closed door is a compromise between total enclosure and open invitation.

Double doors are not restricted to double-sized doorways. In many cases, just a slightly larger than normal doorway might better be fitted with a pair of narrow doors than with an extra-wide, extra-awkward single door that would take up more space than it deserves. Slender double doors can be angled back like a pair of screens, or pushed right against the wall like shutters. Louvered shutters, by the way, make very good double doors. They are used throughout many tropical houses, filtering air and light from room to room, and, with louvers fully closed, controlling the flow of conditioned air. Panels of a beautiful screen, lined with wood, also make marvelous doors. But you must certainly decide first whether the doors are to be open or closed. One woman I worked with made the silly mistake of wishfully thinking she could keep her screen-panel doors closed, so we hung them with the design facing the room. What actually happened was that neither her husband nor any of her sons ever bothered to close those doors behind them, and the poor screens were always slammed back against the wall.

When you decorate doors, the more imaginative you are, the better. You can mirror them, to give the excitement of motion and surprise, and, at the end of a long hall, great depth. You can upholster them with leather or vinyl bordered with nail-heads (if the upholstered door is between kitchen and dining room, interline the leather with felt or flannel—it muffles kitchen noises and helps keep out cooking smells). You can panel a door with fabric or wallpaper. You can decorate it with bamboo or upholsterer's gimp or fancy moldings. Or, of course, you can paint it. Be sure to use semi-gloss paint with matte walls and high-gloss paint with very shiny walls. The gloss makes the doors much easier to wipe clean, and, as every woman knows, even with swinging doors, where you've so carefully attached a protective glass plate, people seem to make a concerted effort to avoid touching the hardware. The French way to paint a door is to have the panels the same color as the room and the moldings a contrasting color. Or you could make a great splashy show of a different vivid color on each panel. Or do as they do in many Latin houses—marbleize the entire door. You can even transform turn-of-the-century glass-paned doors into more modern (and more functional) panel doors simply by painting the glass on both sides.

In a long hall with many doors to closets and bathrooms, it is often wisest to make as little of the doors as possible simply by painting them out. If they are flush doors, you can make them disappear by painting, wallpapering, or even wood-paneling them to match the walls. Of course if the doors are nicely placed, you might want to make them bright punctuation marks in an otherwise drab hall.

When you have limited space, think about sliding doors that slip neatly into wall pockets. Many contemporary houses are virtually doorless except for these hidden panels. For closets where door pockets are impossible, you can have doors that slide on top and bottom tracks (three or four narrow panels are better than two wide ones). Or there are accordion-fold doors, louvered or flush, that double back on themselves when you open them. On a dressing-room closet, I once saw a beautiful accordion door made of slim mirrored panels. Glamorous.

No matter what type of door you choose, be sure it is of the very highest quality —and that it fits properly. I'd rather have no door at all than a flimsy one that wavers or rattles, or sings an aria every time you open it. Doors that swing out over wall-to-wall carpeting must clear both the carpet and its liner, or they'll be a struggle to handle and gradually mow down your rug. Beware, on the other hand, of too-big spaces between door and floor—ill-fitting doors let in noise and odors and wreck the effectiveness of heating and air conditioning. A door's hardware is as important as buttons on a dress. The knobs should be good looking and, perhaps even more important, pleasant to the touch. What they should not do is bite back when you try to use them, nor should they resist. Some knobs are so small and slippery that to operate them you need a pair of pliers.

Then there are those great openings so prevalent in houses built at the turn of the century—doorless doorways leading from a central entrance hall to the various rooms adjoining. At one time a problem, they can be great assets today when a free flow of space is just what everyone is trying to create.

What to make of a wall

Walls seem to be a biological necessity to most human beings. I have visited many modern houses with practically no opaque walls at all, and they are beautiful to see: Outside walls made almost entirely of glass; rooms flowing into each other without interruption. But many people cannot live happily in rooms like that for very long. Sooner or later, up go the curtains or shutters, in come dividers, such as bookshelves, screens, and doors.

It is the walls that run space into a room. When you decide you want a blue room, it's the walls you're talking about. When you want to expand the feeling of space, or to make the room seem cozier, it's how you treat the walls that does the trick. You can make the walls pure background, making them recede into space. Or you can pour on the color and pattern and gleam, turning the walls into the principal decoration, moving them closer to the heart of the room.

Because the color of the walls dictates the color of every other thing in the room, you must feel completely natural and amiable toward it. Wall color, above all else, should never be contrived or chosen according to fashion. You can pick up an extraordinary ashtray or even a little chair on a whim, but the wall color, never. If possible, expose yourself to various wall colors in actual rooms, to see if you really feel more comfortable with brilliant color, dark color, white, or pastels. Remember, however, that walls must suit not only you, but the physical character of the room as well. Is there only one exposure? Then rule out white and very dark colors—lack of cross-light can make them deadly. Shiny dark-brown walls can have a terrific slick city look, especially when combined with lots of black and shimmer. If you want the same dark walls in the country, however, I would use lots of white woodwork and white linen or cotton slippers to add freshness.

When you want a lot of color for the money, you can either paint the room white and have lots of clear-colored cottons on the furniture, or put a clear fresh color on the walls and use patterned cottons with lots of white for even more freshness. When I say clear fresh colors I mean just that—not hard, raw colors. The green of new grass or tender leaves, rather than the somber greens of moss or avocado; lemon yellow instead of harsh gold. Pure clear colors seem to have a wonderful translucency about them. And like white, they can be equally charming in matte or glassy finishes. The paler or softer the color, the better it looks in matte, I think. Who wants to lacquer a daffodil? On the other hand, black and very dark colors must be shiny, or they make the whole room look drab.

I would not hesitate for a minute to paint right over wood paneling, no matter how elaborate it is. Some people revere antique boiserie to the point where they don't dare touch it. I think that's nonsense. Originally it was probably painted anyway. But I would never install a copy of eighteenth-century boiserie—paint is so much more straightforward.

If you want a painted wall with a little extra depth, you can glaze it—first painting it a flat color, then, section by section, coating it with a deeper tone and wiping that off with a brush or cloth so the ground color shows through. The effect is very much like that of antiqued painted furniture. A most traditional combination, originally done in the eighteenth century, is white paint glazed with yellow. But I have gotten beautiful effects with pale pink glazed with raspberry pink, or pale blue over white. "Glazed" is not to be confused with "glossy." If you want the wall shiny as well, you must apply a top coat of clear lacquer.

The most elaborate paint job for walls is, of course, trompe l'oeil. I have two favorite trompe l'oeil rooms: One is a small square entrance hall in a house in France, its walls decorated with vignettes of Persian gardens enclosed in fool-the-eye frames. The other is Mrs. Paul Mellon's greenhouse in Virginia painted to look like a fantasy pavilion with flowers in pots and a low painted wall on which lies a pair of painted gardening gloves. It's a tiny room, and very charming. The danger of trompe l'oeil is that it can get too "amusing." You have to know when to stop.

When you want pattern on the wall, paper is the answer. Wallpaper does not necessarily require pictures as a painted wall usually does. Yet if you do want pictures, a not-too-overwhelming pattern or a small-scale stripe is often a better background for them than plain paint. I love small rooms hung with a big-scale wallpaper, with curtains and furniture covers in matching fabric. Rooms like that have real character. For doors and woodwork, you can use glassy enamel in one of the pattern colors or the background color. For the ceiling, use flat paint in the same color but lightened with a few drops of white.

In England they go in for wallpaper murals, I've never liked them very much, especially the ones that repeat, but there is nothing in the world more glorious than old Chinese wallpaper, which never repeats. Each panel is different, and they hold such a wealth of intricate detail and color you can't possibly take it all in at once. Frequently old Chinese papers are worn with age, but to overrestore one would be a crime. It becomes even more beautiful with the mellowing.

Modern foil wallpapers are great if you want a high-fashion, decorated look, but in my opinion they're not too well suited to home interiors. Sometimes, however, they can be made absolutely marvelous with a glaze of umber. Some old Chinese wallpapers also have silver foil backgrounds, and I would glaze them, too. In fact, I know of one old one that, glazed, became even more glorious then it was originally.

If it's textured walls you're after, look into the vinyls. Some look and feel just like linen, and don't show nail holes. Others impersonate leathers and suedes well enough to fool anyone. You put them up just like paper, but with special paste. And they last almost forever. When your walls are too irregular for shiny paint, you can substitute patent-leather vinyl in brilliant jewel colors. And vinyl is a gift from heaven for children's rooms. For a young boy's bedroom, we chose white woodwork and shutters, and shiny vinyl walls in brilliant electric blue. The floor we covered with an Oriental patterned wall-to-wall carpet in blues and reds and beige. The bunk beds are beige, the bookshelves brass. For a boy of eight, the room is great fun. But the wonderful thing about it is that it will grow up right along with him.

I rarely suggest putting fabric on the wall, simply because there are such fascinating wallpapers around. But if you're in love with a fabric that has no matching paper, there's nothing else to do. I always have wall fabrics backed with paper—laminated—so they can be applied with wallpaper paste. Otherwise you have a great to-do: first covering the walls with clear plastic sheeting, then installing wood strips, then flannel for body, and finally the fabric. Then you've got to go back and cover all the edges and borders with braid.

At the
bottom of every good room
a beautiful floor

When it comes to floors, for the rooms we live in, there are two things I insist on: They must lie down, and they must be quiet. A floor should never jump up at you to the point where people walk around looking at their feet. A floor may be brilliant, but the rest of the room must compensate so the floor is not noticed to the exclusion of everything else. And the clatter of heels on a bare, hard floor can be unnerving.

Making a floor lie down is a fairly recent problem. Up to now people were apt to use patterned furniture, curtains, even walls with a plain dull carpet that seemed almost apologetic. Now we've been liberated. And the person largely responsible is David Hicks, a man who, I think, has done as much for current decorating in England as anyone. His brilliant small-patterned carpets revolutionized the floors of the world.

Small-scale patterns in carpeting not only look more interesting than solid colors, they are infinitely more practical. Even a simple beige and white geometric design shows wear and dirt less than a perfectly plain beige. And don't ever be persuaded that a dark carpet shows wear and dirt less than a pale one—it is absolutely not true.

A personal revolution for me in the last few years has been my conversion to wall-to-wall carpeting. I used to have a terrific aversion to it. I still think that a beautiful bare wood floor with a rug by the sofa or the fireplace is a treasure. It can be any wood, from the simplest board flooring to a fantastically expensive eighteenth-century parquet, imported and assembled piece by piece like a huge jigsaw puzzle. Perhaps because wood was once a living tree, it still has that warmth, that richness, that friendliness about it. Yet I have found that a few small rugs on a bare floor often look like islands, making the room seem restless. I finally had to admit that wall-to-wall carpeting is often the answer. I had it once in my own apartment, and I never regretted it. It was a small dark-brown and beige pattern that smoothed out the whole room and made it a simple matter to move furniture around without having to worry about rug boundaries. I always recommend wall-to-wall for bedrooms in the city, because it helps so much to muffle sound. I've even had a wall-to-wall carpet made out of a too-small rug by sewing a border around it.

A relatively recent concept in wall-to-wall in America is strip carpeting—36-inch-wide sections laid the way they've been doing it for years in Europe. Ever since the invention of broadloom, most Americans would have been appalled at the idea of seams in the carpet. Now we don't think that way at all. My own carpet was in strips, but you'd have been hard pressed to find a seam in it—the pattern hid them perfectly. A while ago I worked on La Fiorentina in the South of France, with creamy marble floors so old they're lustrous without being polished. I had the carpeting woven of beige and white linen and raffia in 60-inch-wide strips. The seams in that were quite obvious. Yet how much more interesting and valuable it is, made painstakingly by hand, than bolts of broadloom produced by the mile.

In the city, I like the warm, deep-comfort look of smaller rugs laid right on top of wall-to-wall carpet. The smaller rug could be a bigger-scale pattern, or one of those bold-colored contemporary rugs, or a needlepoint, or a beautiful Oriental, pale and luscious as a piece of honey.

In the country, or by the sea, the best floors are the most practical ones, and the most practical are often the most beautiful. I love natural clay tile, or slate, or stone and brick—all waxed to a glow. In the country, I think I would tile even the bedroom, then soften it with a lovely pale linen rug. But I would never use brick or slate on the second floor. They suggest an indoor extension of the garden—they seem out of place upstairs.

Almost all of these natural materials—even those wonderful seventeenth-century French floors of slate with bands of wood—have been copied remarkably well in vinyl. I find myself using vinyl more and more. It's wonderful for children's rooms in pale, clean colors. I have put stone-patterned vinyl in a dining alcove, and I once did a whole living room in big vinyl squares that looked just like deep-brown leather. Elaborately patterned floors that used to be done in marble are easily copied today in vinyl. In the Escorial museum in Spain, there is a circular room forty feet across. The floor is beige and green marble with a design that looks like rays fanning out from a central sun. I had that floor reproduced in vinyl in a fifteen-foot circular entrance hall in Lake Forest. Marble had been specified; for a fraction of the cost we made a floor that was quieter, safer, infinitely more interesting.

You can also mimic marble with paint. I once visited a small palace in Scandinavia that had a ballroom on the second floor. Although the plans called for a marble floor, the engineers found it would be impossible—the whole ballroom would have crashed straight through to ground level. So they marbleized it with paint. It was all done with feathers for brushes—a tremendous job. Of course you don't get to decorate too many ballrooms nowadays, but a more reasonably sized room would be beautiful in faux marbre. Or you could have a floor with a painted stencil design—the most beautiful ones I've found are, again, in Scandinavian countries. Many people think a stenciled floor is impractical, but actually the reverse is true. When a stenciled floor is finished, it's given a good coat of varnish. Then you wax it twice a year, and it stays perfectly beautiful. Every floor in every house of Mr. and Mrs. Paul Mellon is painted to resemble parquetry in wood or pale marble colors.

One of my favorite houses is a farmhouse in Connecticut, whitewashed inside from top to bottom. The only rug is a thick white linen doormat. The rest of the floor is completely unadorned except for red clay pots of ivy and geraniums, and big washtubs filled with rhubarb. That house is the only place I've ever felt I could move into—without making a single change other than substituting my own books for the ones that were there—and feel completely at home. In that house the bare floors are the simplest of all—wood, coated with thick, lacquery white paint. It is beautiful to look at and—the ultimate test—it is heaven for walking barefoot on.

To top off
a beautiful room
you need
the right ceiling

I often wonder why even my most sophisticated clients—those who plan a room's colors, fabrics, furniture, and objects down to the last ashtray—so often fail to look up. There was a time when the ceiling was the glory of a room. Think of those beautiful old ceilings in Italy and Spain, arched, sculpted, painted with stars. Or the great English Adam ceilings of the late eighteenth century, elaborately plastered and painted—ceilings so wonderful that carpeting was often woven to match. Today, with some exceptions, the ceiling is largely ignored.

It amazes me that in New York, the tall city with the short rooms, where people ought to be concerned with raising the roof, so many merely give the ceiling a lick of white paint and let it go at that. Unless the walls are stark white, too, white paint is guaranteed to bring that ceiling down all over your shoulders. Indeed, if you really want to lift the ceiling, you should paint it darker than the walls—anywhere from one tone darker to almost black. Then it will recede like a clear sky at midnight and be more dramatic. Many rooms in Latin countries, where plaster-white walls prevail, have ceilings of sky blue or sea green. Not only does the color heighten the room, it also makes the room incredibly cool looking, and helps get rid of that old villain, glare.

Even a room with dark walls can have a dark ceiling if there are enough windows all around to give good cross-light. With only one exposure, though, a dark ceiling can be fatal. A friend of mine once painted his living room, with its single row of windows, a shiny dark brown—ceiling and all. At night it was magic. The ceiling disappeared right into the New York skyline, and the whole room sparkled. But during the day, you would open the door and see absolutely nothing but black, with glare at the far end. It was like living in the Holland Tunnel. My friend repainted his ceiling within a month. It is now a buff color, and that makes all the difference in the world. When a ceiling must be pale, even a few drops of the wall color in the ceiling white keeps the ceiling a comfortable distance away. To raise a light ceiling even more, install a narrow cornice molding painted to match the walls. In small rooms like entrance halls or dressing-room passageways where you don't stay very long, a delightful ceiling raiser is mirror. But I would never mirror the ceiling in a room where you linger very long—it's quite unnerving to glance up and see yourself standing on your head.

There are some rooms, believe it or not, whose ceilings are too high. Generally, the smaller the room, the lower the ceiling should be, to avoid the feeling that you're sitting in the bottom of a well. You can lower the ceiling physically by building a whole new one. One corridor I know has one wall of built-in cabinets, the other of paintings and drawings. The ceiling is unbleached muslin stretched on a frame. And above it, diffused by the muslin's irregular weave, is a row of lights directed at the pictures. That ceiling is functional, attractive, and gives the hall much better proportion. You can also lower the ceiling visually. The simplest way is to paint the cornice molding to match the ceiling, or install the molding a little way down the wall and paint everything from there up in the ceiling color.

Beams in ceilings were once considered such terrible eyesores that they were painted out at once, but they can be great assets. If you have plastered beams, you can wallpaper them or decorate them with stenciling. I've even gone so far as to paint the bottom of the beam pale blue, the sides green, and over each color, thin lines of scarlet. On the other hand, if the beams are only around the edges of a room, I recommend painting them the same color as the wall. They make a kind of frame for the furniture and look built in rather than stuck on. If you have wood beams, you can darken them, lighten them, wax them, paint them, or make them look old and rustic. And who says the panels between beams must be a single color, or even painted at all? One ceiling I know in Peru has wood beams and between them, a herringbone pattern of terra-cotta brick. Another ceiling is hung between pale beams with silver paper, glazed with umber to a bronzed, nonshiny glow.

It is imagination that makes a ceiling, like anything else, something glorious. Recently I worked on one in Florida, a tray-shaped wood ceiling that rose from wall height to twenty feet, with exposed beams crisscrossing one another in marvelous patterns. We glazed the whole thing with clear transparent colors—deep blue and green for the beams, paler shades for the panels between. The result is striking: subtle color plus that beautiful wood grain. In another house I worked on, the bedroom ceiling is dominated by a huge circular skylight. I worried for a while that the couple might be disturbed by the early morning light streaming through, but to my great relief, they love it. Theirs is a living ceiling, thrilling as a thunderstorm, and as romantic as a starlit night.

How to make
a window beautiful

There is nothing as beautiful as a beautiful window, looking out on a country landscape, with filmy curtains blowing in a gentle breeze. A window like that is poetry to a room—gives it movement and life. But even if a window is more problem than poetry—when you need more than a wisp of curtain to control the light, to make the room private, or to reproportion awkward dimensions —the best way to solve it is still with the very least amount of curtain possible.

For instance, I have found that the most glare comes from the top of a window. So if you want to get the most light with the least glare, install a Roman shade or a blind that pulls up from the bottom rather than curtains that draw apart from the center. I have Roman shades in my own apartment—dark brown to match the walls—and my windows need absolutely nothing more. In a feminine room, you could use roller shades covered with fabric to match the furniture, or paper to match the walls, and hang simple curtains at the sides.

I know lots of people who say the most irritating things in the world are those streaks of light that dart through the spaces at the sides of a shade when they're trying to sleep. To eliminate them, have opaque shades or blinds installed so they extend a few inches beyond the glass. To blacken the room completely, hang curtains—lined and interlined—so they completely cover the edges of the shades. All those thicknesses of fabric also help muffle noise.

On the other hand, you might love the light but need privacy. One of the prettiest ways to have both is to install folding, adjustable louvered shutters—one pair covering the top half of the window, another pair covering the lower half. In a bathroom, for instance, you could open the top pair to let in light for shaving or applying make-up and keep the bottom pair closed for privacy. On a wall of windows, floor-length shutters are an elegant change from curtains. Folded back they have almost the same shirred effect as fabric. When they're closed, the louvers temper the light, play with it, break it up, and cast lovely shadows.

Although I do not usually recommend valances, I must admit they help more than anything to reproportion awkward windows, to disguise jogs in the wall, or to bridge two lengths of curtain that are in brilliant contrast to the walls. But a valance must always be the simplest possible and in good proportion itself—a few inches of wood covered with flannel to soften the surface, then fabric. Fat, draped valances always look heavy and self-conscious.

When you shop for a patterned curtain fabric, bunch it together in your hand to see how it will look at the window. Many patterns that are beautiful when straight and taut, look heavy and dense when the fabric is gathered. The best thing to do with that kind of pattern is to cover the furniture with it, but use another, solid-colored fabric for the curtains.

Windows that look too heavy can make the whole room look overburdened. I once worked on a room where a beautiful painting by Goya hung between two windows. The walls were pale yellow and the curtains a very strong dull gold—a color that seemed to overpower that marvelous picture and somehow crowd the whole room. I changed the curtains to off-white, tied back over pale-yellow undercurtains. Just that one change has pulled the windows away from the picture, letting it float and breathe. And the windows themselves are in much better balance with the rest of the room.

Sometimes the best thing to do with a window is nothing at all. One evening I was a guest at a party in the beautiful New York apartment of Mrs. Enid Haupt. It was very high up and overlooked a park. The rooms were filled with exquisite antique French chairs and tables. There was a wonderful eighteenth-century parquet floor, and all around were lots of potted daisies and miniature chrysanthemums that looked as if they'd just been brought in for the night. Through the windows I could see the terrace lined with subtly lighted plants and trees and then the city at night, looking like a thousand diamonds. It suddenly struck me that the most wonderful thing about this room was the absence of curtains that would interfere. In a room where you would expect to find silks elaborately fringed and draped, the window treatment was the simplest, yet most imaginative of all: bare, sparkling windowpanes and a magnificent view. However, as protection from the rain and wind of a stormy night, wood shutters, paneled and painted like the walls, fold over the glass and shut out the tempest.

A HOUSE
THAT BRINGS
THE EIGHTEENTH CENTURY
RIGHT UP TO DATE

What I love about Mrs. William McCormick Blair, Jr., is her extraordinary personal taste and limitless patience. She'll wait for the exact thing she wants, filling in with a plant until she finds it.

What Deeda Blair has done for her Washington house, where she lives with her husband, Bill, and their son, William, is to bring the eighteenth century right up to date. It's like a house a short drive from Paris, which by chance happens to be very near Georgetown.

Genuinely old, genuinely new, or invented, is what Mrs. Blair in-sisted on for every detail of her living room. The plan is for comfort —tables where they are needed, lamps where they are essential, and the colors, except for green table skirts and potted plants, almost not there at all. The creaminess of walls, rugs, and furniture makes a perfect background for people, and for treasures like the phenomenal Coromandel screen Mrs. Blair found in Paris. Since there is no such animal as a genuine eighteenth-century coffee table (Mrs. Blair is an astute scholar of antique French furniture), she prefers to have contemporary functional ones to hold her plants and books. Their slick notes of steel and glass in the creamy room give a wonderful hard-edge sparkle.

She likes furniture, clothes, food, anything at all to be what it is and never imitation. The Louis XV gilt chairs in emerald velvet (so comfortable), Chinese silk-scroll paintings by the fireplace, and the gilt mirror above it, are triumphs of eighteenth-century artisanry. Sofas and the various tables are the best-made, most comfortable contemporaries. All the floors of the house are pale: some covered with five coats of white deck paint, some marble, some carpeted with straw, some, like those in the living room, covered with creamy rugs. "Carpets," Deeda Blair feels, "ought to be absolutely splendid or not noticeable at all." And I quite agree. The most apparent thread that runs through the house is its superb quality. And Mrs. Blair is absolutely correct when she sighs wistfully that the pursuit of quality is endless.

A dining room that doesn't look like one is what Mrs. Blair specified. "Not for me that long brown wooden sideboard, all those straight-up chairs standing around," she said. So the table is a 54-inch circle, always covered to the floor—here in wonderful French hand-painted silk—and surrounded by cushioned eighteenth-century French armchairs. Four matching chairs sit out in the hall, ready to be brought in and set around another table for larger parties. Also in the nondining room, a sofa and chairs. The light in the room is always soft: firelight, candles, sunshine through the shimmering lettuce-green silk curtains, and at night, lights shining softly up through the potted lemon trees. In the marble-floored entrance hall, below, the staircase swirls up to the bedrooms, down to brick-floored sunrooms and playrooms.

COUNTRY HOUSE
IN THE
MIDDLE OF MADRID

What Mr. and Mrs. Placido Arango wanted for themselves and their three delightful children was to have their apartment in Madrid look like a big happy house in the country. The apartment lent itself very well: The rooms are large and airy, with tall generous windows (sliding glass doors in the living room) that overlook the famous botanical gardens. We filled the apartment with old French manoir furniture and sunny country colors, purposely omitting anything massive or heavy looking. The result: rooms that look freshly plucked from some French hillside.

In the living room, with its shining fruitwood floor, the walls and curtains are a beautiful warm pearl gray—a color sadly neglected here in the United States. Two small sofas are slipcovered in gray, apricot, and yellow cotton; a table is skirted in blue. Everything else is tawny: the two lovely Tibetan rugs, a big beige linen-velvet sofa, the patterned cotton on the open armchairs. Most of the paintings in the room are Spanish: Some are by Sorolla, who painted in the early part of this century; others are by contemporary painters—Tapies, Michaux, and Gen Paul.

*T*he yellow dining room, left, *is splendid simplicity: yellow cotton table skirt, white cotton curtains, wonderful brown and white geometric rug. But it's anything but conventional. First of all, there isn't a sideboard in sight. Instead, two little console tables hold vases of crab-apple branches, heavy with fruit. On the wall facing the windows is a contemporary tapestry by Antoni Clavé. But the real glories of the room are its over-mantel picture, a portrait of St. Thomas by El Greco, and the dining-room chairs—an unbelievable set of twelve Louis XVI gilt armchairs, covered in leather.*

The library, above, taller than the other rooms, is lined with tortoise-shell vinyl and banked with books. By the fire, on top of the dark-brown geometric carpeting, is an antique Moroccan fretwork rug. Across the room, a French game table. The painting over the mantel is a Bernard Buffet.

You can create
a personal atmosphere
almost anywhere.
With the stamp
of your own personality
your house won't be
a carbon copy of
any other in the world.

6
DECORATING FOR FOR HOW AND WHERE YOU LIVE

When Mrs. Gilbert Miller wants to live off the cosmopolitan stage for a time, she leaves her Manhattan apartment or London town house or English country house and heads for her holiday villa in Mallorca, shown here and on the following four pages. There, a complete change of pace. Leisurely. Relaxed. Involved only with close friends who also delight in clear skies, calm waters, the refreshment of informal living. Architect for the main house and guesthouse was José Alcover. The decoration is a gathering of antiques, local handcrafts, and furnishings from the U.S.A. intended to promote the insouciant mood that draws Mrs. Miller back to this blue haven.

THE REFRESHMENT OF INFORMAL LIVING IN MALLORCA

The great pool and the deep Mediterranean blue beyond are the whole point of the house. Much of the day is spent in, or at least overlooking, the water. Spanning most of the main floor is an open loggia, left, with sitting and dining areas, flanked by curtains of duck to be drawn against the evening breezes. Just inside the loggia's glass doors, the dining table, below, is set for a midday meal.

*W*hite, black, and straw in the living area of the marble-floored loggia, above, *are doused with flares of color in the flowers, the pillows, and the topiary ficus trees. The plaster table lamps, lacquer coffee table, and wicker sofa and chairs are all American. The little straw chair in the foreground is from Spain. Above the sofa, a still life by the English painter Brooker. The guest book,* left, *conveniently placed on a table near the living room entrance, is surrounded by a charming still life of Mrs. Miller's treasures: seashells, an ostrich egg on a gilt bamboo stand, a summer bouquet, and on the wall a vignette of the sea. In Mrs. Miller's bedroom,* opposite page top, *the bed and its masses of scalloped pillows are all covered in flowered cotton. On an English lacquer cabinet nearby, a collection of brilliant blue opaline glass. An upstairs guest room, all snowiest white, has a simple little writing table, charming pictures, and a silk-embroidered pillow with Elsie de Wolfe's famous motto, "Never complain. Never explain." But its greatest decoration is the glorious view of the sea. In the neighboring guest bathroom, walls are hung with the most charming patterned tiles, made in Mallorca.*

A HOLIDAY HOUSE IN OLD SAN JUAN

When Woodson Taulbee found his wonderful old eighteenth-century house on a cobblestone street in Old San Juan, it was a mud-floored structure in terrible disrepair and utterly devoid of the simplest necessities. But the foundation was sound and the thick walls and ceiling beams built to last. Mr. Taulbee gutted the house and, as part of a government-sponsored general-restoration program, rebuilt the interior, keeping to the flavor of the period when the house was in its prime. He installed marble floors, wrought-iron grillwork at windows and porticos, and filled the house with cool open-work furniture.

Intricately carved teakwood furniture, made in India, presented to Queen Victoria, is now lacquered white for the Woodson Taulbee living room, left. Reflected in the mirror above the sofa, twin elephant sconces from the Brighton Pavilion. There is Spanish iron in every room: here, a wall lantern and a terrific old weathervane, long as a lance. The entrance hall, above, is a mixture of nationalities: king-size Spanish lantern, an extra-long Italian bench, a pair of Venetian monkeys at the doorsides, and an early eighteenth-century English painting of a huge hound. Outside, right, the house is charmingly situated on its cobblestone street in Old San Juan.

Designed for coolness in the Taulbee dining loggia, above, the furniture is openwork rattan, cotton covered, the principal decoration is a contemporary painting and a series of elephants.

*O*ff *the old courtyard is the kitchen—a perfect spot, with its view through arching doorways of rustling greenery. In the old Spanish lantern, a bird makes its nest each season—a lucky omen!*

Upstairs from the kitchen, iron-grilled arches, opposite page left, *open from the guest-sitting room,* opposite page right, *where the airiest wicker furniture surrounds a needlepoint rug. In the guest room, an oval opening,* left, *is filled in with a wrought-iron fish —to discourage visiting pussycats. Near the tall window in the master bedroom,* right, *a writing table and bench, antiques from Spain.*

It's a polished Florida technique: hot-weather architecture (the "Florida room" exists far beyond the state). Here, in the James Fentress house, we took all the cool thought of Florida architect John Volk—deep galleries, colonnades, open patios—and gave it international echoes, bright rumors of tropical, colonial, hotland houses all over the world. The polished red-tile floors, the shutter-shadowed windows, the thin blowing curtains in wide-opening walls—hints of Morocco, Mexico, Spain. Mr. and Mrs. Fentress have deliberately left the options of illusion open: Neither stringent nor overblown, their house rises as if on a private island with nothing to stop the eye but a perimeter of green, and in one direction, the Inland Waterway, in another the sea.

A FLORIDA HOUS
WITH A
SUPER COOL LOO

Like a temporary tent that someone might have pitched for the weekend, the guest room, opposite page, was designed as a flare of Indian colors, but with coolness always in mind. The beds are covered in bright quilted cotton and set on a canopied platform carpeted in cotton. The living room, above, took its cue from the colors of straw and rattan, all tans, white, and black, in naive printed cottons. In the master bedroom, left, all persimmon and white, the two enormous beds are swarms of butterflies. The sitting-dining room, left, was made doubly cool-looking with darkbrown printed vinyl walls, pale cotton on the furniture, and a ceiling painted mauve. The house's entrance, below, is dramatic at the end of its courtyard tattersalled with grass.

Nothing is interesting
unless it is personal.
If you really like
something,
you can usually find
a place for it—
but maybe not the one
you had in mind.

7
YOUR OWN PERSONAL STAMP

YOUR OWN PERSONAL STAMP

Nothing adds more
to the warmth and personality
of a room
than objects you love

Whenever I work abroad, I am struck by the Europeans' love for objects. They have a passion for little things they can strew like jewels around the room, and they find great pleasure when traveling in discovering some new treasure to take home with them. I often wish objects held more of a fascination for Americans, for they are the most intimate, personal part of decorating. There is nothing that adds more to the warmth and personality of a room.

So important are objects that when I take a client shopping for a table, I always look around the shop for some vase or clock or sculpture to put on top, so we can see what the table looks like adorned. A table is, after all, meant to hold things. No matter how beautiful it is, a table is positively forlorn with nothing on it. A room full of empty tables would have about as much charm as four blank walls.

I couldn't bear living in a room without objects all over the place. It gives me the greatest pleasure to glance around my living room and be reminded by a brass turtle of the friend who gave it to me, or by a funny old stone ball with white enamel facets imprinted with numbers of the curious English shop where I found it. (Your guess is as good as mine as to what it could have been for.)

I do not mean you should run out and buy a bunch of little boxes or sculptures or brass turtles just to fill your tables. Ludicrous as it may sound, I know people who actually do that. One woman I know bought a truckload of cheap imitations of those beautifully designed, fabulously expensive eighteenth-century gold boxes and arranged them on library tables as if they were museum pieces. That is the height of pretension and the lowest form of fashion. What I do mean is that people should keep the objects they love out in the open where everyone can see and touch them. Or, if they have no objects to speak of, I'd like to see them begin to notice bits of fine craftsmanship, or some interesting texture, or even to find beauty in an object because of its history. There is something very appealing about picking up a cut of rock crystal or a piece of Inca gold and holding it for a bit in your hand.

You could have anything that fascinates you—a collection of minerals or archaeological finds. Or things you remember noticing on your parents' living-room tables

Overleaf: A breakfast bar in the sawmill guesthouse of Francis L. Kellogg.

when you were small—those indescribables of no intrinsic value but great personal meaning. It doesn't matter how much money the object is worth or whether it is beautiful or an utter monstrosity. The only thing that matters is the joy it brings to you.

It is difficult for some people, however, to tell whether what they see will be a lasting joy or just an ephemeral whim. Especially when you travel, it is sometimes very tricky to choose among native pottery or weaving or what have you. Remember that many of the designs have been altered or updated in some way to please tourists. They are not really very good in their natural surroundings, and when you get them home they're horrors. Unless native crafts have very beautiful, classic lines, they often do not travel well. When you put them in your living room, you find they look vulgar, and they cheapen the things around them.

Many people, as they accumulate things, just mix them together any old way, assuming that any sort of hodgepodge on a table will turn out all right. They are dead wrong. Some combinations of objects look just as heavy-handed as argyle socks with evening sandals. A striking piece of Mexican pottery, for instance, might be wonderful with an inlaid wood box, but when you try to put it near a piece of delicate porcelain, the porcelain looks puny, the pottery ungainly.

In his small house in the South of France, Roderick Cameron has filled every table and chest with the most beautiful objects arranged in the most striking ways. On one table he has surrounded a perfectly wonderful Greek marble foot with a group of pottery boxes and animals, all made by a very talented potter who lives nearby. They are all strong, although they are small. They are weighty. They have immense dignity and enormous character. On another table is a collection of hands—stone hands, glass hands, porcelain, metal, and wooden hands, hands of all sizes and attitudes. Here he has mixed the delicate with the massive. What makes them happy together is their common subject. When this man arranges a table, he does it with the care and critical eye of an artist making a collage—and is just as absorbed in his work. I've watched him put a group of things together, take something away, replace it with something else. "There's only one way to tell what goes together and what doesn't," he once said to me. "and that is to try them." Trust the logic of the eye.

I have found that in general certain things do mix well. Tortoiseshell and wood, for instance, concentrated together on a single table, look much better than if you scattered them around the room. It's really the same principle as planting a garden— a sprinkling of red tulips throughout the garden hasn't one tenth the impact of one glorious mass. Another way to mix things is by the quality of their color—the pale off-tones of a miniature Monet painting, for instance, alongside a pink-marble Greek sculpture and a pale-green shagreen box. Or an Imari bowl together with a red-lacquer box and a bunch of tiger lilies.

Don't forget plants and flowers—they mix with anything. It seems the presence of a growing, living thing on a table makes everything else come alive, too. But the same rules apply: With a table full of pottery and pre-Columbian artifacts, you would use a small flowering cactus rather than a bowl of roses.

Once a woman who had just been married asked me to help her arrange the things she had brought with her when she moved into her husband's apartment. When I got there, waiting in the middle of the living room was a card table absolutely jam-packed with boxes, sculptures, minerals, and all kinds of curiosities, all of them very dear to her. She was more than a little worried about putting them around the room; her husband was a man of great taste. He already had a great many very beautiful things, which he had arranged with obvious care. One by one, we added the objects on the card table to the meticulous arrangements around the apartment. We put her gold boxes with his gold boxes, her Greek marble with his Mesopotamian sculptures. We covered nearly every square inch of one table with their tortoiseshell collections. The woman also had some very fragile feminine things that couldn't very well go in the living room or library, so we grouped them on a glass table by a chair in the bedroom. When the card table was empty, I said to the woman, "Now the most foolish thing you could do is start your life together with a quarrel over these objects. If your husband thinks the room is a mess, or if he feels he has been invaded, simply take everything off. They can be put back later, a little at a time, so they can be absorbed gradually." She called me later that evening to tell me her husband had loved everything—"it was as if he had arranged it all himself." I know how strong and how personal the love of objects can be. If those two collections were so well mated, I can only conclude that their owners, too, are living happily ever after.

One of life's great pleasures is living with the pictures you love

It has been said that Billy Baldwin has the worst paintings in New York. From an art critic's viewpoint, I suppose it's true. My pictures are curiosities rather than great art. Yet each one means something special to me. And I love them.

There's no denying that very good pictures are symbols of status and often wise investments as well. I know of one drawing by Matisse that was bought for $850 in 1949 and sold this year for $15,000. What other investment in the world could net that profit? But when someone quickly shows you the signature on a painting and tells you how much it's worth, you know he hasn't much feeling for the painting itself. And I don't think anyone has the right to possess a painting he doesn't love.

I would never insist that a client buy a certain picture just because I liked it, any more than I would give a picture, sight unseen, as a present. A painting is a wonderful gift as long as the person has seen it and is dying to own it.

But I have seen people give paintings to suit no one's taste but their own. They think they're generous. I think they're insulting and intrusive and should be severely punished. Even if you fall head over heels for a painting, remember that love at first sight does not necessarily mean love forever. A beautiful painting hanging in the gallery may look entirely different once you get it home. Even the gallery owner knows you must live with it for a while before making a decision.

The wonderful thing about buying pictures today is that you can get good art at affordable prices. I love people who buy different kinds of pictures by unknown artists. As they grow more knowledgeable and discriminating, they weed out earlier purchases and develop greater sensitivity to quality. And there's the delightful bonus of chancing to hit on a real winner, delightful not because of the financial rewards— you probably wouldn't want to part with the painting anyway—but because you've recognized lasting worth.

No work of art should ever be regarded as decoration. When you try to fit a picture into a room by color or subject, you reduce it to the level of a chair or wallpaper. When you try to glorify a painting you love by contriving a whole room around it, you often suffocate it instead. I tried it once, taking as my color cue a very pleasant picture of a young girl in lovely shades of apricot, pink, and blue. We covered walls, furniture, and floor in the same warm glowing colors. But when we hung the picture, it counted for absolutely nothing. The room drained it of all its life. It can happen, of course, that a painting you love is by chance in the same colors as the room where you plan to hang it. I once did a room the color of raspberry ice with flowered chintz of pinks, oranges, and yellows, then found, by sheer luck, a huge abstract by Stamos in exactly the same colors. For another room, a town-house guest room wallpapered with Nantucket wildflowers, my client found a perfectly beautiful still life of fruit by Bonnard that picked up every tone in the wallpaper. No one will believe the rooms came well before the paintings. Yet if you think about it, you see that probably we would never have chosen those room colors if we had had the paintings to start with.

If you really love a painting, you can usually find a place for it—but maybe not the one you had in mind. Several years ago I worked on a monochromatic room completely steeped in shades of icy blue—walls, fabrics, rugs, everything. One day the owners called me to see a new picture they'd put over the mantel. My reaction was instant shock. There before me was a rare Rembrandt—a very dark and somber portrait of a miserable-looking old man. It had profound power, but the atmospheric quality of the blue room made it look almost frightening. It looked as though we had kicked a hole in the wall and there was a dungeon next door. I persuaded my clients to move the Rembrandt to their wood-paneled library, where surrounded by books and dark leathers it was absolutely glorious.

There is a fashion today for having a great many pictures all over the walls. I have found that some rooms do indeed look wonderful with lots of pictures, but there are still one-great-picture rooms. Sometimes it's best to leave a wall entirely blank. Many young people with no pictures to start with find it a great temptation to fill every space at once. I always tell them to wait until just the perfect pictures come along. Then, too, you can fall in love, as one of my clients did, with space. Five years after working on her living room, I discovered what I thought would be the perfect picture for over the sofa. But she wouldn't hear of it. "I'm happy with nothing on that wall."

When I'm rehanging a client's collection of pictures, I almost never return them to their original places. Two that might have been rooms apart often take on new vitality when hung side by side. Pictures scattered about the old rooms sometimes look more connected in a single grouping. Or one small one from an old group could be a little jewel hanging on a space alone. I have also found that pictures moved from a large house to a much smaller apartment often look friendlier and more relaxed in their reduced circumstances. Moving day, by the way, is a good time to reassess the value of your pictures. There is no reason to keep a painting you've outgrown, or really don't care for anymore. But don't make the mistake of sweeping too clean. Your pictures are a bigger part of your life than most people realize. More than anything else in your new house, they can make you feel instantly at home.

The best places to put pictures are the unexpected ones. I like the idea of taking a typical over-the-sofa painting and hanging it out in the hall, where you can get up and go see it rather than sit in its shadow all the time. I love to see little pictures hanging on bookcase dividers, or standing on the shelves alongside the books. In one room I backed a picture with plywood for protection and stood it in a window. In my own apartment, I have a painting on a floor-standing brass easel. And of course there are those beautiful tiny pictures on easels to stand on tables all around the room. Photographs look wonderful stacked and plastered all over very small personal rooms. Not brides or Sunday-best studio portraits, please, but snapshots of houses you've lived in or of the kids tumbling over a haystack. It's rather like leaving the family album open for everyone to see—and just as charming. One of the most beautiful arrangements of pictures I've ever seen is a collection of Bonnards hung on the wall of a stairwell. They had been removed from their heavy gilt frames and hung utterly unadorned against a background of mushroom-colored toile de Jouy—just the way Bonnard himself often hung them in his own studio.

There was a time when all the paintings in a room had to be framed exactly alike —in those very heavily carved gilded wood Barbizon frames. Today each picture is framed—or not framed—according to its individual personality. There is no reason, for instance, to keep a frame around a picture just because the artist—even an old master—put it there. Very likely if the artist were alive today he'd change it himself.

In general I like less frame rather than more. I have an enormous pastel of a lion in a very dark brown and tawny beige, so yawning and wild that it would be inhuman to trap it in a frame. Another of my paintings—a small old Dutch oil—needs its broad, dark wood molding almost for protection.

When it comes to lighting a picture, I advise you to forget all the silly rules people have devised about always lighting from above, or always from below. Lighting, like framing, depends on the picture. Sometimes just a table lamp placed nearby is enough. Some pictures need uplight, others can't stand anything but daylight. The most expensive lighting for paintings is a tiny pinpoint in the ceiling, far enough away and carefully masked so the softest light exactly frames the picture. But no matter what kind of illumination you use, the final goal is always the same: light so subtle that the painting seems to glow on its own.

The best decoration in the world is a roomful of books

When I was young, I used to find great pleasure in imagining myself sitting at the head of a great big double bed in the middle of a huge room, completely surrounded by books. My real-life room and bed are considerably smaller than I used to envision, but the books are there. Books are my constant companions and my best friends. If I suddenly came into a lot of money, I think I would spend it on travel and books—books I've had my eye on but have considered extra luxurious, books to give as presents to my friends, and, for my own old favorite books that are dog-eared and worn, brand-new bindings.

Bindings are a very extravagant luxury, but there are some books I am so fond of—decorating and architecture books and even some fiction I've read several times—that I feel they deserve as beautiful a place to live as I can possibly give them. Each binding should suit the contents of the book. For instance, I see a book on Louis XV decoration in a baroque color like red or orange, one on Louis XVI in a classical green or blue. I have seen only one beautiful instance of a collection of books bound all alike. A Greek scholar I knew had all his old classics rebound in vellum that varied in color from pale cream to the amber tone of honey. Never, never would I have matched bindings by the yard. I hear some people even buy their books by the yard,

177

never reading a word of them. They might just as well put up plywood panels covered with backstraps. People who simply do not read should fill their apartments not with books, but with evidence of their interest in other things.

My one contribution to the actual design of furniture was the set of brass bookcases I made for Cole Porter's apartment, and which I also have at home. Perhaps it is significant that I did not design something to sit on, or to have dinner at, but something to hold books. Bookshelves should be a matter of thought and imagination rather than expense. Of course you can have brass, glass, or solid oak, but you can also buy shelves by the mile of plain unfinished pine from the carpenter or the department store. You can have them finished in any color lacquer, or covered with leather or rattan, or marbleized. You can paint them yourself, or edge them with tooled leather. My one piece of advice: the more the better. I love to see doors and windows completely surrounded by bookshelves as though someone had cut openings right through the wall of books. I love to find, every time I visit a family, a few more little bookshelves that have sprung up since the last time I was there. Books will grow in a house like a vine if you provide something to support them.

Breakfronts make beautiful bookcases, especially the big ones that look built-in. I know a small library on Long Island that was actually constructed around two enormous antique mahogany breakfronts—shelves above, cabinets below—that extend almost the entire length of two opposite walls. Their fronts are flush with the walls, which turns their bulk into great depth. What I don't like are books arranged in breakfronts with porcelain birds and Lowestoft plates. That reduces the books to mere decorative objects, which I think is criminal. I don't think bookcases should have glass doors either. In a French room I might reluctantly allow grillwork, but generally I think you should be able to read a title from across the room, and take a book down instantly, without the nuisance of opening a door. If the books are old and rare and fragile, by all means put them behind glass—and keep the door locked. They are not everyday reading matter, in this instance, they are treasured possessions.

I love to see books piled on tables, but I don't mean those coffee-table books that people get as presents, then go mad trying to figure out what to do with. I've actually seen stacks of them used in a living room as tables, complete with candles. Imagine what would happen if you wanted to take one of those books out and look at it. What I do mean are piles of books to read, to use, to refer to—like the ones Pauline Rothschild has stacked around her bed.

How exciting it is to visit someone and find the book of the moment—politics, ecology, whatever—right there on the living-room table. It might be the one open current from the outside world in an otherwise peaceful retreat. But it charges the whole house with energy, and makes for instant conversation. You can carry even this pleasant idea to extremes, however. One brilliant English decorator used to keep a basket by the sofa filled with a bargain-basement pandemonium of the latest books. She called it keeping abreast of the times. I call it showing off.

There isn't a room in the house—including the bathroom—where books aren't first-class decoration. I can't imagine a guest room without at least one small bookcase, or if there isn't enough room, shelves built in under the windows. Good guest-room books could be volumes of current short stories, or best-selling paperbacks you can lend without worrying about their return. I never lend hardbound books I love unless I'm sure the borrower will treat them with respect and be meticulous about returning them. The replacement copy of a book that has been lost just isn't the same as that original familiar volume.

Rooms for books aren't necessarily pine-paneled "dens" anymore, nor need they have dark-walnut walls like those in traditional town houses. Bedrooms and dining rooms are being turned into libraries. Other people plan serious libraries, with walls of books to the ceiling, library steps, and a table in the center. And they make sure there are enough comfortable chairs to read in—or have dinner. I have friends whose large entrance hall stretches to the left and right of the front door. They have lined each wing with floor-to-ceiling bookshelves and placed a great red-lacquer table in the middle.

When you decorate with books, no room color is wrong. In very small intimate libraries I lean toward the deep, rich warm colors. But pale ones are also beautiful, as they are in La Fiorentina in the South of France where the library was designed as a cool, quiet room. Its walls are strié the color of straw, the furniture is a yellow and green print, the windows overlook a grove of olives. I know another library—in Mrs. Wintersteen's Pennsylvania farmhouse—that has pure white walls and a Scotch-plaid rug, with scarlet furniture and red-flannel curtains. In winter, it's the coziest room in the world. I would never have dreamed of a blue library, but in the Chateau Mouton-Rothschild the lofty library walls are all painted a deep, soft blue, the furniture is blue velvet, and the shelf sections are divided by vertical beams marbleized in blue. The books—of every color imaginable—just sit on their shelves and glow.

How to enjoy
your family photographs

It seems odd that we Americans, enthralled as we are with the idea of commemorating every occasion with photographs, often wielding the camera ourselves, hardly ever, after we've got the pictures, know what to do with them. I go into a grandmother's living room and find, framed on the piano, a picture of her as a bride thirty years back, or on the wall, a row of stiff studio portraits looking unbelievably uptight. All the casual snapshots we take on vacation or during happy days with friends get stuck away in boxes or drawers waiting to be glued into albums. And that's too bad, because those little informal photographs are often more valuable than costly art—not in artistic merit, but in what they mean to us, and in what they can do to make a room unmistakably ours.

Snapshots mix well with formal portraits of graduates or brides, with watercolors done by family members or friends, with a little child's portrait of the family dog, even with little drawings or prints you've picked up during your travels: One couple I know has collected a veritable diary of their life's adventures in the small drawings and prints on their walls—each one provokes its own set of memories, growing dearer to the couple as the years pass. In such a group you might even include some extraordinary Christmas cards or letters from friends. All are happy together because they are all very personal indeed.

As a general rule I think a group of photographs and memorabilia hung together belongs in a small intimate library or study. In a more formal living room, or hall, I would put family pictures on easels on tables, or hang them very casually on the upright supports of bookcases—even a tender sprinkling of them can break the hard formality of a big room. On occasion, however, an ordered potpourri on the wall can give a small living room great depth and warmth. Such a grouping can also work very well in a narrow hallway, but never up the stairs. It's unfair to the pictures to try to appreciate their small and interesting details while balancing on one foot.

Recently I worked on a house in Washington belonging to a couple who had spent most of the past ten years in diplomatic service in Europe and Asia. The house was typically Washington, with a central hall opening onto living room, dining room, and library. The first three rooms were all done in clear, fresh gardeny colors, with lots of white and leaf green. But the library was to be a more masculine room, very personal and quiet, where the husband could receive his official callers. One wall was lined solidly with books. There was a fireplace in an adjacent wall, and along the other two, we put comfortable sofas and good reading lights. Among the books were several large, bound scrapbooks that contained part of a vast collection of photographs the family had accumulated during their assignments abroad—personal family pictures, group shots of the family with business associates, or remarkable, informal photographs of U.S. presidents the man had known or worked under. To make the room masculine, yet still related to the rest of the house, we painted it the shiny color of a well-moistened leaf plucked from one of the living room's ficus trees. To make the room personal, we turned the three bookless walls into an open photo album.

You must have a system for hanging photographs on a wall. For that room in Washington, the couple first sorted through what must have been thousands of pictures, keeping for the library only the most treasured. These we divided into groups—one of family records, another of times shared with friends, another of the events of a particular assignment, and so on. Each group became a panel of pictures—one the length of each sofa, two others to fill the spaces flanking the fireplace. The only rules we followed from then on were that all the bottom and topmost pictures were to be approximately level. For the chimney piece we saved the most public of the pictures—magnificent ones of Churchill and the presidents—many my client had taken himself.

Apart from subject matter and the top and bottom boundaries, everything about the groups was absolutely nonuniform. The frames were a positive hodgepodge, although none was elaborate. Most were narrow strips of black, white, or dull gold. To have the frames all alike, I think, would have given them to much importance. Varying them made them seem insignificant to the point of nonexistence. But don't forget they were hung on a background of dark green, a color with character and deep perspective. On a white or pale-colored wall, I would try to match the frames—perhaps just simple narrow wood strips painted black or one clear color—to anchor those little pictures and give them greater definition.

Some of the pictures had mats, some didn't. We kept the mats with inscriptions, for that, after all, is the final magic that makes a mere photograph a treasure. Even the shapes and sizes of the groups themselves were not intended to be static. In fact, I expect those pictures to spread like espalier trees, eventually joining one another to fill the entire room.

Before you drive a single nail, you should arrange all the pictures on the floor. I usually begin by putting the largest one near the center as a hub, then work outward from there. When they're all down, you just move them around as in some kind of giant game until you have a pleasing arrangement. I usually put high-contrast pictures or close-ups or faces at the top, and those intricately detailed group shots, and of course anything with writing, down lower where you can see them without straining. Don't even attempt to make the margins around pictures all equal. In the first place, unless the pictures are exactly the same size, it's futile, and in the second place, some pictures need more breathing space.

When you have all the pictures the way you want them, measure with a ruler from the bottom frame of the lowest picture to the hub picture, then from the sides to the hub, and transfer the measurements to the space you've planned for them on the wall. Hang the hub picture. Then, again starting from the center, hang the rest. You may find, especially if the ceiling is high, that your angle of perspective is much more acute than when the pictures were on the floor. To adjust for this, you simply allow more space between the higher ones.

Can you imagine what happens to a whole roomful of featherweight photographs in flimsy little frames every time a door slams? That problem can be neatly solved by using a tiny nail at each side of the hanging wire instead of a single one in the center. I find those two little nails are better than one special picture hook—they keep everything pancake flat.

Finally, after you've made all the last-minute adjustments and have stepped back to admire your work, take all the pictures down again, one by one, and number them left to right, top to bottom. I'd even make a small numbered schematic drawing to match, and keep it in the safe.

The filtered glow of an English country house—clear, keyed-up colors and day-long floods of sun—gave this great-roomed city apartment that belonged to Cole Porter a quality of detachment from city life. (Actually it was in the tower of the Waldorf-Astoria Hotel in New York.) The graceful curving French furniture, which filled the rooms, came mostly from Mrs. Porter's superb collection bought for the Paris house on the Rue Monsieur, where the Porters lived in the 1920's. (A clustering point of expatriate gaiety, the house was the scene of—among other epic events—the first Charleston lessons.)

COLE PORTER'S COUNTRY HOUSE ON
THE 33rd FLOOR

*B*rass bookshelves—*my most en during design—were created fo Cole Porter's study, above. Thre tortoiseshell walls are banked wit them, and they are filled with one o the most remarkable libraries I hav ever seen. Here, at the big writin table, is where Cole wrote all hi scores, although the pianos are out i the drawing room. (The Porter wa was to write words and music straigh through before playing a single note. A rare Chinese bird, painted in th early fifteenth century, hangs over sofa in this entrance hall, right, whos walls and ceilings were marbleized i the warm shades of milk and honey The floor, laid over acoustical mu for soundproofing, is a herringbon beauty from an old French house Through the door is the dining en of the drawing room.*

The wallpaper is the dazzler in the Cole Porter drawing room, where astonished birds and magnified butterflies hover among branches of intense yellow lemons and bright, bitter oranges on a pale-oyster ground. Designed in the late seventeenth century, when other wallpapers ran mostly to florals, it came from the famous English country house "Knole," the seat of the Sackville family. The extraordinary Louis XV sofa against the right wall and two painted and whiskered Régence sofas came from the Porters' own house in Paris. The treasure of the room is the floor: Parquet de Versailles, laid over acoustical mud, with a patina that can actually be felt through a thin shoe. Most of it we left beautifully bare, with three smallish rugs, Spanish and old, marking the main furniture groupings.

COLE PORTER'S COUNTRY HOUSE THAT CLIMBED A HILL

The view of the Cole Porter house, *left,* is an artist's, and this page, *above,* a photographer's view. But what the sketch shows better than anything is the esthetic result of a house-moving: a small cottage that inherited the site, cellar, and formal gardens of a large outdated house—and made them its own beautifully. The cottage began life as Cole Porter's workroom, about 600 feet down the hill from the main house. When it climbed the hill (not completely under its own steam—three dollies and a 20-ton truck provided wheels), it claimed the glorious view of Greylock mountain—one of the buying points when the Porters first saw it in 1940.

Every room breathes in light and air—and good deep breaths at that, drawn across the Massachusetts Berkshires. Surrounding the cottage, top, *and its formal lawns and gardens, are clipped mountain meadows and trees that stretch far and away in all directions. Just visible through the trees to the left is the wing added by architect Jack Coble as Cole's bed-sitting room. Inside, masses of flowers fresh from the cutting beds that dot the grounds fill the rooms at every eye level—sometimes as many as five or six bouquets to a room. The Scottish housekeeper used to fill the old house's rather dark rooms with color-by-flowers, and continued the practice in the cottage, though there, there was not a shadow of a darkness to dispel. In the living room, the chief concern was with comfort: good deep chairs, functional reading lights, a special alcove for the extensive record collections and for the record player with its hookup to the bedroom loudspeakers.*

*T*hree Mary Faulconer vignettes of Porter lifestyle: top, ferns for the piano, a bowl of potpourri on the television set, roses on a nest of lacquer tables. Above left, a lemon tree in a wicker basket in the sunny gallery that connected the original cottage and the added wing. Above, a supply of pencils (points down meaning time to resharpen) in a seventeenth-century coconut cup, and garden flowers in Bristol glass.

We'd come for coffee and stay forever in Cole Porter's bed-sitting room, opposite page. It comprised most of a new wing and was easily the most charming room in the house. Nine months out of twelve a fire burned in the fireplace under that Greek head (breezes are chilly at 1500 feet). Two of the walls were lined with books—so completely that the windows look as if they had been chopped through. The remaining walls were of white brick, a wonderful background for Cole's Chinese screen, a French desk in a satiny wood the color of honey-gold, and those Porter chairs, covered in a stripe of strong yellow cotton to match the bed, which we designed just for this room. Here, too, were all Cole's indispensables: the flowers and plants wherever you look; the pencil pots; and the ubiquitous wastebaskets.

SAWMILL GUESTHOUSE
WITH AN
AFRICAN BEAT

To convert the old tumble-down sawmill on his 100-acre homestead in New York State, Francis L. Kellogg worked for two years with architect Marsden London, always careful ·to preserve the mill's authentic charm. The mill sits on a jut of fieldstones at the brink of a millpond, *above*, full of reflections, snapping turtles, and all manner of transient geese. Inside, we decorated it with all the tawny colors and jungly textures we could find, as a showcase for Mr. Kellogg's wildlife trophies. One of the mill's nicest features is all that light and air that soars clear to the ceiling, a phenomenon brought about by the removal of one of the old lofts.

*T*here are eight different patterns in the living room alone—geometric variation of zebra stripes, leopard spots, cobra scales—not counting the genuine articles. Even the ancient beams, dark and rough, form a geometric fretwork on the stark white walls and ceiling. The vinyl floor is colored and textured like an elephant hide; beige sofa and armchairs are edged with embroidered leopard spots.

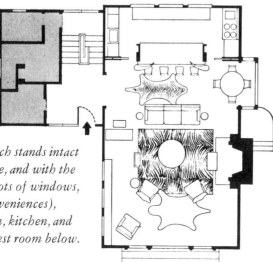

The original mill, which stands intact (sans loft and sawblade, and with the addition of fireplace, lots of windows, and a few modern conveniences), consists of sitting room, kitchen, and bedroom loft, with guest room below.

*T*he miracle of the Kellogg millhouse is the lighting, all designed by Wilson Skewes. He spent hours cutting templets for sunken ceiling spots so the light would trace the outlines of various objects on the walls. A pair of giant elephant tusks, left, forms ivory parentheses around the chopping-block counter, also used as a breakfast bar, which divides the sitting area from the kitchen. For parties, a louvered screen hidden in the ceiling can be pulled down to block off the kitchen and make the living-room half of the counter into a buffet. Above the kitchen, the tiny loft bedroom has a center wall panel that slides down to form a window overlooking the lower level. Across the kitchen, enormous glass doors, all of which open onto the fieldstone platform, give the sensation that the mill-pond is not merely a vista, but an inherent part of the room. The French country chairs at the breakfast bar can be used to augment seating at the dining table, below right, set in a newly built bay window just a splash and a gurgle away from the waterfall, which makes wonderful background music for lunch or dinner.

ART
EVERYWHERE
YOU LOOK

When I first saw S. I. Newhouse, Jr.'s New York penthouse, there were only a few modern pictures on the walls, the roots, I was told, of a collection that was to grow and grow. My job was to provide a calming, undemanding, yet comfortable, livable background for a budding garden of art. There were two requirements: that the furniture plan not have to be altered as the collection grew (pictures, of course, are constantly shifted about), and that nothing detract from the brilliance of the art. I felt somewhat like a landscape architect who must keep in mind how the flowers will look when they bloom, so he won't overplant. The decoration, therefore, is of the greatest simplicity. There is no bold color anywhere. The living room is full of whites and naturals, airy, open, lighted by a huge window with a skyline view, cut through a wall of books. For the more intimate rooms, I thought dark, rich colors would be more inviting and comfortable than relentless white. But even there, the furniture blended into the background like foliage, leaving all the glory to the art. The interesting thing is that as more and more paintings have been added, the apartment has somehow become less and less overwhelming, so you are not instantly dazzled by any one thing. Instead, the paintings make a kind of extraordinary pattern, weaving the rooms together into a fascinating, highly personal whole.

The living room is a white shell, intended to be hospitable to paintings and sculpture as well as to people. Mr. Newhouse's requirements were "comfortable furniture, but nothing with too strong a personality of its own." So we filled the room with a blend of natural textures, and so kept everything visually undemanding to let the wonderful paintings have all the deserved limelight. The rug is pale straw, loose-cushioned sofas are covered with beige cotton, ottomans are suede, blinds an unusual cotton stripe. The excitement is in the art: Barnett Newman's "The Word" above the fireplace, Morris Louis's wall-filling canvas, a David Smith sculpture behind the sofa, and up on the ceiling, a painting by Alexander Liberman. Two small Snelsons flank the fireplace, a Ruth Vollmer is on the coffee table.

194

*E*very inch of wall is tapestried with paintings; every change of perspective makes the room seem somehow new. On one side of the room rise the green shafts of a steel sculpture by Anthony Caro. Across the room, beside an arched doorway to the hall, glows a lighted cage of concentric cubes by Leroy Lamis. Above the arch, a deep-blue and red Clyfford Still, and beside it, a tall red-white-and-blue Frankenthaler. Beside another archway hangs a black and white painting by Jackson Pollock; above it, a flaming Kenneth Noland. On the table beneath the enormous Louis, a Mark Di Suvero sculpture; under the table, an Isaac Witkins. None of the art is spotlighted. Mr. Newhouse enjoys the subtle differences he sees as the room light changes.

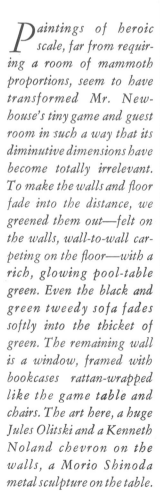

*P*aintings of heroic scale, far from requiring a room of mammoth proportions, seem to have transformed Mr. Newhouse's tiny game and guest room in such a way that its diminutive dimensions have become totally irrelevant. To make the walls and floor fade into the distance, we greened them out—felt on the walls, wall-to-wall carpeting on the floor—with a rich, glowing pool-table green. Even the black and green tweedy sofa fades softly into the thicket of green. The remaining wall is a window, framed with bookcases rattan-wrapped like the game **table** and chairs. The art here, a huge Jules Olitski and a Kenneth Noland chevron on the walls, a Morio Shinoda metal sculpture on the table.

A brown-velvet-papered cave, Mr. Newhouse's bedroom is a handsome background for paintings by Mark Rothko and Morris Louis. Rich colors can make wonderful backgrounds for art at home—the paintings and sculptures seem to be very much at ease here. Also in the room, a Barnett Newman lithograph and a Paul Feeley sculpture. Except for a low bookshelf, a couple of bedside tables, and the huge bed, the room is devoid of other furniture.

The wilder the idea,
the newer,
the farther out,
the more it demands
that you know
why you want it.
If you fall in love with
something,
that's all that matters.

8

THE BIG
QUESTION
OF
CHANGE

THE BIG QUESTION OF CHANGE

The fashion
versus
what you like

Never in my life have I seen people experimenting with so many marvelous, courageous ideas as they are today. It's a healthy time for decorating. Everyone is so uninhibited. Everyone has learned so much about color, furniture arrangement, paintings—the works. Since I first came to New York in 1935 the level of taste has zoomed.

At the same time there seems to be a craving for drastic change, and that, to me, indicates not health, but a great restlessness. I have always believed a room should begin beautiful and grow more so every year. Change for change's sake puts far too much emphasis on fashion. Too many people are afraid to do anything that isn't currently in style. To them decorating is some sort of status symbol. It's not so much that they are in love with their fashionable and expensive signed French chairs or steel and plastic sofa, as that they think they're supposed to be. The tragedy is that frequently what they had before was much more charming.

When you come right down to it, fashion is merely the result of promoting a good idea—an idea that originally was unique and personal. Rooms filled with pattern-on-pattern, for instance, may be the biggest thing going now, but I've been doing my own version of it for years.

Back in 1933, Ruby Ross Wood decided to do a dining room in brown and black and white—a color scheme unheard of at the time. After searching for months, she found one fabric in black and brown—a wonderful plaid made of horsehair— that she used to cover the dining chairs. To get a beige tablecloth she had to dye it herself. For curtains, she had a fabrics firm do a special print—a pattern she found on a fabric in a museum. It was a flowery chintz—creamy roses, beige-y roses, black leaves, brown leaves. When everything was done the room looked marvelous. And absolutely unique. Five years later, everyone in the world had black, brown, and white rooms. Today, of course, it doesn't take that long for unique ideas to become popular. But there is still that important distinction between having something because it's you and having it because it's In.

Even when your slipcovers or rug have worn out, that doesn't mean you have to replace them with something different. If the colors and designs create just the right atmosphere for you, what's wrong with simply duplicating them?

Adhering strictly to fashion can lead to regrettable mistakes. I used to know a

206

Overleaf: A corner for conversation in the London living room of Mrs. Gilbert Miller.

woman who was very rich, very old, and very fat. Everyone called her Mrs. Bassinet, because she tried to compress her 300-pound self into chic Paris dresses designed for lithe young models. She just couldn't see the difference. In decorating, the difference is not always so obvious. Often a woman will come to me saying she's wild about a certain room and wants one just like it. But as we talk, it begins to dawn on her that she is going to be living in that room, and she really wouldn't like to.

Sometimes people crave change out of sheer boredom. I can understand that. "I'm just so tired of it all," they say. "Can't we please do something different?" Excitement is what they need—a psychological lift. In my mother's day whenever a woman felt low she went out and bought a new hat. Now people are using their moods as excuses to get a new room. That's pretty extravagant.

Recently somebody asked me, "Are you against change, then? If you do a room for me, must I have it for life?" Well, of course not. But some things are for life. When you spend a great deal of money on a priceless antique armoire, for instance, or custom-made upholstered furniture, or one of those outrageously expensive supermodern chairs, that's for life. I like to see good, healthy, constructive changes. Like having four sets of slipcovers to switch around when the spirit moves you.

Every change you make—especially major ones—must be for a reason. When I taught at the Parsons School, I found I had to justify everything. It's not good enough just to have this year's colors and this year's designs and this year's fabrics. You cannot give in to caprice. And the wilder the idea, the newer, the farther out, the more it demands that you know why you want it. You must test the sincerity of everything. Look selectively at what you see. Ask yourself, "What will I think of it three years from now?" Will you love it just as much, or will it be something you can hardly wait to get rid of? One of the worst sins you can commit is to spend too much money on a whim—"a conversation piece."

On the other hand, if you fall in love with something, that's all that matters. Your love protects you from all upsets. Sometimes someone will say to me, "How could you let Mrs. Jones keep that awful picture?" Or worse, they will say to Mrs. Jones, "Surely you're not going to have that." But Mrs. Jones will have it, because she loves it, and will love it regardless of what others think. By the same token, you should never have to invite outside opinions. Nobody ever asks, "Do you really like it?" unless he himself has a serious doubt.

The sad truth is that most people buy something not because they love it, but because they think people will notice it, or talk about it, or—more important—talk about how daring they are to have bought it. And that is what works against them. You should never be so aware of a room that it comes between you and the person you're with. That's not decoration, it's interference.

I'd love to see less and less studied decoration and more and more things chosen because you love them. That's the whole point, really. Having the colors you love. The fabrics you like best. The furniture you find comfortable. In a word, the things that matter. To You.

CHANGE
TO MAKE A ROOM
FOR LIVING

I t's hard to believe that Mrs. Gilbert Miller's big beautiful living room in London was once forsaken, except for big parties, in favor of a small library. To make it more livable, we closed off two tall windows on one wall to cut the room's length and make more room for furniture. We curtained the others in creamy raw silk to match the horsehair-covered walls. Off-white and brown wall-to-wall carpeting also deemphasized the room's long thinness, made the arrangement of meant-to-be-moved furniture more flexible. There are two main groups of furniture in warm ambers: a corner banquette by the fire, right, a sofa group, left, across from the windows. Beneath the mirrored panel on the far wall, left and above, is a lovely Régence commode inlaid with tortoiseshell and mother-of-pearl. A picture by the contemporary English painter Brooker hangs above the banquette. All the pictures are Mrs. Miller's very personal choices, and she did the needlepoint herself.

A ROOM THAT GROWS
LIKE A GARDEN

*M*rs. Clive Runnells and I began her living
room overlooking Lake Michigan twenty
years ago, and it is still not finished. The basic floor
plan has never changed, nor the color of the walls, a
pale gray-white. What has changed, in a slow steady
bloom, is the quality of her possessions and the brilliance of color. Mrs. Runnells is a collector, and
every few years replaces a piece of furniture with
something rarer or more beautiful, or adds a superb
mirror or a painting—a Pissarro, a pair of Cana-
lettos. She has given her room the care and thought
that all great English country houses are given. She
has cultivated it like a garden. And what great garden ever remains static? Not one.

Mr. and Mrs. Lee Eastman have in their New York living room a magnificent collection of paintings by Rothko, de Kooning, and Kline. Until recently the room was the usual gallery white, with sofas and chairs covered to match the paintings, and the Eastmans hated it, never went into it. "What we want," the Eastmans told me, "is a room for us alone and for us with people, beautiful by day or by night." The biggest step toward filling that order was to change the walls to glossy brown vinyl, a beautiful unifying backdrop for paintings and people. Everything else is noncompetitive but deeply comfortable. We grouped seating around a beautiful Oriental rug: for entertaining, a corner banquette in cut-linen velvet; for intimate sitting, two sofas in pale Siamese pink silk. At night, screens covered to match the walls unfold to block out the window. The room looks as if it had been there forever.

FOR GREAT MODERN PAINTINGS, A ROOM WITH A PAST

INDEX

N

NEWHOUSE, *S. I., Jr., 194, 196, 198, 200*
Penthouse (1969), 194-201
  bedroom, 200-201
  game and guest room, 198-99
  living room, 194-97
NEWMAN, *Barnett, 194, 200*
NOLAND, *Kenneth, 196, 198*

O

OBJECTS, *25-26, 172-74*
  see also PERSONAL COLLECTIONS
OLITSKI, *Jules, 198*
OUTDOOR ROOMS, *59-61*
  trees and plantings for, 59, 61
  see also TERRACES

P

PAINT, *93-94, 136-37*
  choosing colors, 136
  glazing, 136
  trompe l'oeil, 136-37
  see also COLOR
PAINTINGS, *11, 20, 62, 174-77*
  arranging, 176
  backgrounds for a collection, 46-47,
  97, 194-201, 212-13
  buying, 175
  finding a place for, 175-76
  frames for, 176-77
  in hallways, 44
  lighting for, 114, 177
PALEY, *Mr. and Mrs. William, 98*
Sitting room (1963), 99
PALLADIO, *Andrea, 80*
PARISH, *Mrs. Henry, II, 45*
PARK & TILFORD, *15*
PATTERN, *26, 101-102, 104-105, 137*
PAUL, *Gen, 148*
PERSONAL COLLECTIONS, *25, 62, 160,*
  172-74
  arranging, 173-74
PERSONAL TOUCHES, *172-81*
PHOTOGRAPHS, *176, 179-81*
  hanging and arranging, 180-81
PICASSO, *Pablo, 12, 94, 118*
PICTURES, see PAINTINGS
PISSARRO, *Camille, 210*
PLANTS *(indoor), 121, 173, 188*
POLLOCK, *Jackson, 196*
PORCELAIN FOOT WARMERS, *48*
PORTER, *Cole, 9, 13-14, 24, 105-106,*
  116, 178, 182, 185-88
  Country cottage (1957), 186-89

  bed-sitting room, 189
  exterior, 186-87
  living room, 187
  Waldorf Towers apartment (1955),
  13-14, 105-106, 116, 182-85
  drawing room, 184-85
  entrance hall, 183
  library-study, 105-106, 182
PORTER, *Linda (Mrs. Cole), 14, 182*
POTTER, *Pauline Fairfax, 12-13*
  see also *Rothschild, Baroness*
  Philippe de

R

REMBRANDT, *175-76*
RENOIR, *Pierre Auguste, 23*
ROMAN SHADES, *60, 142*
ROOM DIVIDERS, *45*
ROTHKO, *Mark, 200, 212*
ROTHSCHILD, *Baron Philippe de, 58*
ROTHSCHILD, *Baroness Philippe de,*
  12-13, 23, 58, 178
ROUND HILL CLUB, *9-10*
RUBINSTEIN, *Artur, 24*
RUGS, *108-109, 125, 138-39*
  Aubusson, 56, 108
  Bessarabian, 26, 93, 108
  Karabagh, 35
  Moroccan, 48-49, 108, 133, 151
  needlepoint, 164
  Oriental, 26, 108, 213
  Samarkand, 108
  Spanish, 184-85
  Tibetan, 149
RUNNELLS, *Mrs. Clive, 48, 132, 210*
Florida house (1959 & 1965), 48-49,
  133
  foyer, 133
  living room, 48-49
Lake Michigan living room (1972),
  210-11
RYAN, *Anne, 84*

S

SCREENS
  Chinese, 64, 189
  Coromandel, 132, 144
  Korean, 67, 96
SECOND HOMES, *156-57*
SEVIGNY, *Charles, 82, 117*
SHINODA, *Morio, 198*
SHUTTERS, *48-49, 92, 134, 142*
SITTING ROOMS, *52-53, 99, 119, 165,*
  167, 189
SKEWES, *Wilson, 193*
SLIPCOVERS, *22, 63, 94, 98, 126*
SMITH, *David, 194*
SNAPSHOTS, see PHOTOGRAPHS
SNELSON, *Kenneth, 194*